Children *of my* Choosing

Children
of my Choosing

memoirs by Bruce Fraser | *edited by* Kathleen Fraser

First edition, 2010

©2010 Bruce Fraser
Isla del Sol
Shawnigan Lake, BC
Canada

Children of my Choosing
ISBN 978-0-9866350-0-7
Editing, design, layout, and production by Kathleen Fraser
Cover photograph of Lara Fraser by Bruce Fraser, ©2010

All rights reserved. No part of this book may be reproduced in any form by any electronic or mechanical means (including photocopying, recording, or information storage and retrieval) without permission in writing from the author.

This book was printed and bound in the United States of America.

Contents

Children of My Choosing ... 1

i. definitions
Tenderfoot ... 5
The Making of a Queen's Scout ... 9
Molotov Cocktails and Cornish Game Hens ... 13
Black ... 17
Cain's Discovery ... 21
On the Green Chain ... 23
By the Merest Thread ... 27

ii. influences
Ring and Tone ... 33
Battlefield Promotion ... 35
Appeal Court ... 39
Two Nights Before Christmas ... 43
Just in Time ... 45
The Blewett Watershed ... 47
Crusader ... 51
Landing or Not ... 55
The Waters Close ... 57

iii. adventures
Attack of the Fungi ... 63
Your Daughter is a Bright Young Girl... ... 69
Fire Drill ... 73
At the Feet of the Mighty ... 77
Zim Dollars ... 81
The Mango Tree ... 85
How To Break In a Pathfinder ... 87
Lara of Africa ... 91
Saying No to Noor ... 95
Last Day in Jordan ... 97
Going to the Wall ... 101

iv. reflections
Air Raid ... 107
Estimates of Calibre ... 117
Hello Nose! ... 119
A Tryst at Noon ... 125
A Ghost at the Reunion Table ... 129
Landfall's Last Sail ... 133
The Moral Majority ... 137

Children of My Choosing

Children know only a small part of the inner lives of their parents. They know what their mothers and fathers did for them and gave to them. Often they know how the formal opportunities of their lives were provided—their education, their engagements in sports, music, art, technology or work. They remember the rules they lived by and the enforcements or inducements by which these were delivered. They remember the social atmosphere of their childhood. They remember the celebrations, the cookies, the casseroles, the board games and the camping trips. Commonly, they attribute both their good fortune and their misfortunes to the environments that their parents created. At worst, they cannot muster gratitude and become estranged. At best, they truly understand the nature of loving sacrifice and remain close. It is the nature of things that the young must focus on their own trajectories in launching their lives.

Later in life, too often at funerals, we look back on our parents' lives through a mist of our own making, remembering highlights but not always substance. We can render their deeds but not their thoughts. We can remember well how they related to us, but not always how they related to the issues of their own lives. This natural way of things is vastly amplified in the blended families of our time. Children of rearranged parents are, quite naturally, even further removed from intimate knowledge of their new guardians. An even greater gulf can be expected to arise from the planet-wide mixing created by the intertwining roots of ever-multiplying international and cross-cultural adoptions.

Add to this the influence of social media and the instant communication among friends and pseudo-friends—the youth of our day are eternally wired to each other's passing thoughts. Ear buds have become the essential badge of the connected. The force of conformity to ever-changing custom, the engineering of thought with the pressing demands of consumption and the dissociated world that these forces may create shrink the small, inner thinking space that the lives of parents might once have occupied.

I am not indulging in the typical intergenerational complaint about the decay of today's youth. We were not any different and they are not decaying. They are facing their own era with as much gumption as any generation that preceded them. I am simply recognizing that in every generation the young are preoccupied with their own developing lives and that in the emerging realities of today's world the growing number of second-hand parents don't occupy much space.

I do not have children of my own making. I have a doubly blended family, an adopted daughter from one marriage and three stepchildren from another. I chose all four children as deliberately as I chose to be married to their mothers. What follows in this book is a set of tales that my four chosen children have never heard and a point of entry to my own inner life. So Lara, James, Alexander and Emily, here I am.

i *definitions*

Isla del Sol, a quarter-acre island in Shawnigan Lake, was purchased for my mother in 1927, when she was 12 years old. She was recovering from a bout of scarlet fever and needed a place to recuperate. Her grandmother and mother thought that the island would be a perfect place to camp in the warm days of summer. When she was a teenager, her mother contracted Tony Darcy to build a cabin that still stands, a 1930s vintage structure, his first building. Tony became a successful contractor in Victoria and has long since retired, but his first building remains. On my twenty-first birthday, at the cabin dinner table, she handed me the title deed to the island and the life of a sovereign. If you are thinking of how to invest for your children's future, be informed that the island was purchased from the E&N land grant for $200.

Tenderfoot

My first pair of caulked boots was a more important measure of arrival at manhood than my driver's license. They were of hard leather with a fringe at the tongue, leather laces and a spectacular set of hard steel teeth. They were also at the cheap end of the spectrum of logger's boots, a fact that was to become quickly evident in the bush. Much later I would graduate to Paris or Dayton's but the cost of those would require a bigger paycheque and a lot more experience. We tied them with a secret knot that wouldn't catch in the underbrush. I was two inches taller and clumped authoritatively when I walked.

Scoutmaster Adams had arranged for me to join a Forest Service road location crew at Cottonwood on the road to Wells-Barkerville in the summer of 1956. I had the sinewy title of "axeman-chainman" which meant in practice that I was the advance man chopping aside the thicket of devil's club for the compassman. I learned that even the standard thick bush pants with a rubber inlay were not enough to repel the twisted revenge exacted by devil's club stalks. They didn't do all that well with rain-soaked bush either. Knees usually became a pincushion of festering needle marks. These were signs of the experienced bushman, of course, and an object of rueful pride and comparison back at camp.

The next most important instrument of pride was the Hudson's Bay Axe: a two-and-a-half-pound head, sharp as a razor, with a short, light hickory handle. It would cut the alder and brush—and, for the unwary tenderfoot, boot toes—like butter. After the evening ritual of plastering dubbin on caulk boots, using the heat of the gas lamp to drive the stuff home, I discovered that even a lot of dubbin does not stop water getting in those axe cuts!

Sharpening a Hudson's Bay axe was another satisfying camp ritual. After the mountain of grub, in the fading light, the axeman would see to his tools. First, I'd cut a wedge shaped notch in an aspen, drive the axe head in backwards, and file the edge—coarse first for the rock chips then draw file it smooth—then I'd turn the head over, drive it home, and file the other side. The steel of the axe took on a very fine edge. Just as I completed this operation one evening, someone called from another tent. I looked up; the axe came loose at that moment and dropped in a perfect arc onto the arch of my left boot—just like butter. I had another slice in the boot but this time I also had one in my foot.

Our bush camp was a five-mile hike from the nearest road, part of it along the top of a twenty-four-inch placer pipeline, and the camp boss decided that I needed stitches. The hike was out of the question so I was bundled onto one of Ski Prosser's pack horses and trundled down to the Wells-Barkerville road and into a clinic in Quesnel. Three stitches (and an extra visit to the steam bath) later and with a suitably affected limp, I was back on the horse and returned to camp. So what does a convalescing axeman do while he heals? Chop wood for the camp cook, of course—but that was with a splitting axe, which just doesn't compare to the Hudson's Bay.

Ski Prosser had been a rancher and horse packer till his stained Stetson and his faded denims looked like they had grown on him. He was bush wise. His answer to a sliced foot was a bit different. He carried a vial of purple potassium permanganate crystals with him. He demonstrated one day with a cut to his hand: pour the crystals into the cut and let it foam for a while. When the blood-permanganate mixture dries, you have a perfectly cauterized and sterilized wound. This was pretty impressive, as was the resulting scar. I might have been interested in that if the cut had been on a part of my body that would have been visible to the girls back home.

As it was, the beard would have to do.

The Making of a Queen's Scout

"I'm in jail, could you come see me?" The distraught voice at the end of the line was, totally inexplicably, that of our revered scoutmaster. He was our mentor, our teacher of skills, our campmaster, our role model. Disbelieving, I hurried down to the old stone building on Fisgard Street, the forbidding police headquarters in Victoria. Just inside the door was a window through which I asked the officer on duty where he was being held. "Over there, in the drunk tank," was the reply. The tank was just across the foyer, a large holding cell with a heavy wire screen looking out—there he was, his hands clawing the wire, and in the background a gaggle of drunks barfing their way to tomorrow's release into the streets. I spoke to him briefly but it turned out that release on the morrow was not to be for my mentor and friend.

"A misunderstanding involving one of the boys," he said, "not a justification for me being in jail—can you help me? My fiancée is coming next week, she doesn't know anything yet... what am I going to do?"

So I began to enquire as to what lay behind his sudden trip to Victoria's holding cell. One of the boys had broken down in front of his father, revealing that he was sexually involved with the scoutmaster. This explained his increasingly disturbed behaviour around the home and sent his father flying into an immediate towering rage that led directly to the police and a quick arrest. This was in the fall of 1958 and there was no room for nuances: little counseling was offered to either party, there was no restorative justice, the law was strict and the scout leader was before the court within a week. The judge did not hesitate for long: "Abuse of a child by a man in a position of trust... six months in Provincial Prison, take him away, case closed!" Thus ended a scouting career and a life of adulation from boys and parents alike. In 2010 we are dealing with such a backlog of hidden or ignored cases of such abuse, it is significant that the justice system acted with dispatch in this instance. For six months I got letters from "Drawer O," which was the address for the dreaded Okalla Prison. It was hard to write sympathetic letters back. I was dealing with the fallout. I was the eighteen-year-old troop leader that inherited leadership of the boys and a moral challenge of major proportions.

When the boys got wind of the circumstances they at first blamed their troop-mate for their revered scoutmaster's imprisonment. He was shunned and could not return to the troop meetings. The boys were confused about who the victim was, scoutmaster or boy scout. We were all victims in different ways, and I had to do something to heal the troop.

So I gathered the boys around the campfire circle and began, "There is good and bad in everyone, and sometimes one gets the better of the other. Our leader has good qualities as well as bad ones. He has given us much and we do not need to throw that away. He made a terrible mistake for which he is being justifiably punished, but his positive gifts to us as a scout leader are still valuable. Our troop mate is also a good person, and he is suffering because he was led astray and he needs our help. We need to bring him back to the troop and support him in this difficult time."

One day I presented this case to Dr. Geddes, my professor of psychology at Victoria College, and asked him for advice about what I was doing to heal the troop. He said that I was doing the right thing. But more, he expressed his amazement at how youth were facing the great questions of life, even at my young age. It humbled him, he said, but he was already humble, which is why I approached him in the first place.

What transpired was that our troop-mate was invited back. Courageously, he came, and the boys accepted and supported him. I became the official scoutmaster of the troop. We all grew. He went on to excel, becoming a Queen's Scout in due course, proving that good can prevail over the worst of circumstances if we are careful to acknowledge the good while rejecting the bad.

As for the man, he eventually came out of prison, his fiancée waited for him faithfully, they married and he went on with his life. I met him and his bride at their small house in Victoria, shortly after his release. He was bitter and that was the only time I saw him. It seemed he felt that there was a miscarriage of justice—that the punishment, a sentence that stripped him of his avocation and that would follow him forever, was unequal to the crime. There was no compassion for the boy, no regret for his impact on the rest of us, no sense that there was an obligation to be served. I could not reconcile this, could not renew a friendship. For me and for the boys he was lost to time and may, sadly, have never closed this chapter in his life with the courage displayed by a remarkable boy and his mates.

Molotov Cocktails and Cornish Game Hens

Ian McTaggart-Cowan, the famous zoologist, dissected his bird perfectly, leaving a meticulously arranged and correctly sequenced pile of well-cleaned bones. Mine, not quite of specimen grade, was a jumble of disconnected ligaments and flaps of torn skin with the appearance of a recent road kill.

As President of the UBC Graduate Student Society I was sitting at Ian's right hand, entertaining the Dean at our annual banquet. Pleasant speeches were given, plans for an expanded Graduate Student Centre were broached, and the state of the university was discussed in general terms. Nothing was said that might have foreshadowed what I was soon to discover just down the road in the 16th Avenue bush!

I had double-booked myself. I had promised the West Point Grey Scout Troop a camping weekend on the University Endowment Lands while also forgetfully arranging the annual banquet for the same night. Duty demanded that I meet both commitments. So, with only mild trepidation, I took the troop out to camp on a sunny Friday afternoon, raised the tents, found water, set up a campfire and made an early supper followed by mugs of hot chocolate. Things were just as they ought to be. Waving farewell, I set out to preside over the seven o'clock banquet on the UBC campus. "See you at 7:00 in the morning," I shouted as I disappeared down the trail, looking over my shoulder at the fading evening light, the circle of happy faces and the campfire smoke drifting gently into the trees.

I will never know how long it actually took for that group of uniformed and disciplined campers to be transformed into Lords of the Flies! The evening passed, the Dean took his leave, and I slept well anticipating that I would have to roust the boys out of their sleeping bags when I joined them on Saturday morning.

As I entered the 16th Avenue bush trail I had to pass a concrete-covered reservoir. Out on the pad was a pile of scorched, broken glass. "Vandals," I thought, shaking my head as I hiked past. Just down the trail were two overturned shopping carts. "Typical." I muttered as I stepped around them.

Further down the trail I met an agitated member of my troop. "They are going to get a gun," he shrieked, and my calm expectation of a camp of sleeping boys evaporated in a stomach-churning instant. I found the camp in turmoil and a wild story bubbled out of the now assembled, very much awake, circle of boys. It all started—shortly after I left—with a trek back into civilization to collect bottles and two cans of gasoline, which they transported in the borrowed shopping carts. Molotov cocktails were constructed and exploded on the concrete surface of the reservoir, accounting for my observations on the trail.

After the flames died down and the excitement dissipated, the group looked for more unsupervised adventures. They discovered that another scout troop had set up camp a short distance away and had also been left by their Scoutmaster to enjoy the night on their own. I don't know what his excuse was.

A raid took place by flashlight. The rival troop's tent ropes were cut and my tribal marauders retreated under cover of darkness to their own tents. At first light the reprisals came. They cut our tent ropes, slashed the tents with knives and drove blades through sleeping bags, narrowly missing sleeping boys. Two groups of Lords were now in full cry as the conflict escalated. One boy in the enemy troop noticed in daylight that his group was generally smaller and younger than my crew so he sent for an older brother to help balance the scales. He told our boys that his brother would soon arrive with his .22 rifle to pay them back.

I hastened over to the rival camp, arriving at the very moment that the gun-toting older brother stepped into the woods. He was taken aback at seeing an adult who was going to spoil the retribution. He hesitated long enough for me to grab the rifle by the barrel. I ejected the chambered cartridge, broke the rifle over a stump and threw the parts deep into the bush. The rival group gathered their camp remains and I sent our crew home as fast as possible. Some of the language used was unbecoming of young gentlemen.

For a year afterwards the Scouting establishment in Vancouver debated the well-distorted facts, swapped accusations, tried to apportion blame and contemplated disciplinary action. But in the end it all faded into folklore. After all, no one had actually been shot.

Ian had no inkling of the dark side of that evening. His calm authority and complete grasp of the ceremonial occasion would not admit of the chaos just down the road. If he detected any nervousness on my part that evening he could only have attributed it to my youth and inexperience, or perhaps my botched dissection of the game hen alongside the Master's superior performance.

Little did he know.

Black

A thought—*I hope he's not on my crew*—ran through my mind unbidden when the small black man appeared in the gang of new inventory teams assembled at Green Timbers.

It was the spring of 1959. We had all been selected by the Forest Service to be partners in two-man forest inventory teams. When we first arrived at Green Timbers in Surrey we had no idea with whom we would be paired. I reacted with dread when I saw him, an ignorant reaction I was later to eat with relish.

Once the teams were identified (he was with another partner, to my relief) we were briefed on our summer task and issued our field equipment. For a nineteen-year-old forestry student, this was a stock list from nirvana. It started with a land rover, a windowless van, a three-section pack boat with a 5-horse Martin outboard, a 30-foot riverboat with two 25-horse Johnson outboards mounted on a trailer towed by the land rover, tents, cooking gear, maps, data sheets, aluminum survey markers, axes, chains, first aid kits, ropes and, intriguingly, a two-way field radio contained in a green wooden box. There were also hints of helicopters, Beaver flights to remote lakes, bear stories, fishing stories and one man who was packing a Colt 44 magnum in a belt holster. I was primed for adventure.

My team was slated for Quesnel Lake and the wilderness beyond, hence the incredible list of land and water vehicles. His team was also headed up the Caribou highway but to a position south of us at Canim and Horsefly Lakes. That meant we were to caravan together up the highway. I considered it a close call.

I was given the land rover to drive, towing the 30-foot riverboat trailer. OK, I had forty-five minutes' experience in a rover when I was seventeen, but none at all towing a trailer. I had to ask where the starter was. It was a button under the dash carefully concealed by those insane British makers of car wiring—Lucas was their name, which in time became an electrical epithet. That made me lag a couple of minutes behind my new team leader. I made it out of the Green Timbers compound, turned in the direction I thought they had said they were going and a half hour later was intercepted just before the American border by my frantic partner in the van. Eventually the caravan made it to the highway up-country and I grew used to grinding noisily along at 40 mph, top speed. But it was macho—nothing like it on the road.

Coffee and lunch stops were frequent. My black colleague began to emerge: a UBC Aggie from Trinidad, product of a mixed East Indian-African marriage, with a wild sense of humour, West Indian rhythm and a penetrating philosopher's mind. By the end of the trip I was a bit sorry to see him leave the caravan for his assigned territory. The two crews were to stay in touch, however, as part of our field safety procedures was a nightly check-in by radio with HQ in Kamloops and with our nearby teams. "XMO67, XMO67, this is XMO84," we called to his camp. We would set up the radio aerial by wrapping the wire around a soup can and chucking it over the highest branch we could find. "Hi guys, you OK, over."—"Rained like a bugger today, over."—"Up the north arm tomorrow, over and out." Not much for erudition, but friendships grow in strange ways.

Sometimes the crews would meet on a weekend to compare the inventory process, tell tales and unwind after slogging through the rain forest, measuring tree diameter and height, estimating defects, plotting the sample sites on maps and stapling markers on the key trees. There is nothing quite like arguing in the rain about which ridge you are on when the air photo is blurred, your boots are soaked and supper is a long trek away. These weekend visits led to a growing friendship as I slowly moved toward colour-blindness.

In the fall of 1961 I visited my good friend Hollis Kelly in Port of Spain, Trinidad. I stepped off the Super Constellation into the steam of the sub-tropic night, drove past the smoking garbage heap and its denizens, turned eventually into a hibiscus-lined driveway and was poured into bed, albeit with a small draft of rum. Trinidad was the Caroni Swamp Bird Sanctuary with its flocks of scarlet ibis, it was the tar pit at San Fernando, it was Callaloo soup in a family kitchen and it was nearly being run off the road at Caracas Beach by a pickup driven by the Mighty Sparrow and his calypsonian friends. It was limbo in the clubs, soursop milkshakes and endless idealistic discussions about how to develop a country.

But, it was also one memorable trip to the small interior town of Couva. Hollis paraded me up the main street—me in my white shirt, white shorts and white skin. Trinidadians are not shy: they laughed, they poked, they felt, they laughed some more. Kids trailed us, people crossed the street for a first hand look. The word 'conspicuous' comes to mind!

Hollis said, "Now you know what it is like to be black in Vancouver."

Cain's Discovery

I fell through the floorboards onto packed dirt that had not seen daylight since 1913. The embarrassment of a dinner guest up to his knees in floor was nothing compared to the manic laughter of the cabin's seventy-year-old builders. "That floor has been wanting to do that for fifty years, you know see," said Cain, as he helped me onto firmer boards. Fortunately the planking under the table was firm enough to support the cauldron of moose stew and dumplings that lay on the other side of the jagged hole.

Mike and Cain Oknianski, brothers from Galicia, rafted down Francois Lake in 1913. They built a log cabin on the south shore of the lake and began the arduous task of clearing pasture on the 750 acres they claimed for their homestead. Spruce, pine and aspen patterned the rolling hills of their land while the cabin looked out on the three-quarter-mile shore of the lake. Between 1913 and 1962 Mike and Cain had cleared one hundred acres of pasture, run cattle, built barns, and logged a few of their trees, but had never touched the cabin they had built that first year. I'm not sure that they ever fixed that hole in the floor—too many other things to do, and you could just walk around it.

The brothers were the most colourful characters in the tiny community of Tatalrose. Checked shirts, suspendered pants, fractured English, manured boots and legendary good natures made them both instantly recognizable and always welcome. They were never apart and tended to finish each other's sentences in a tumbling flow of homestead wisdom, local gossip and current news. What was less known about them was that their otherwise sparsely furnished cabin held a storehouse of books. Mike and Cain were avid readers, precisely up to date on politics, philosophy and affairs that seemed very far away from the southside communities of Tatalrose and Grassy Plains, where I was teaching school on a letter of permission.

In brilliant sunshine, after the instant arrival of spring in a single day on the twenty-fourth of May in 1963, I was manoeuvring among my grade seven to ten classes in English, Social Studies, French, Music, Physical Education, Home Economics and Woodworking Shop—all subjects for which I had been qualified by my two years of forestry at UBC! I was in the midst of a breathless class in abysmal French to the students of grade eight and distracted slightly by anticipating what I was about to say about the fall of Rome to the other half of the room, which housed restless grade sevens, when the door of the classroom burst open.

In swept Mike and Cain waving a book! "You have to read this right now, you know see, you know see," said Cain in high excitement. It must be pretty important to charge right into a teacher's classroom and interrupt such august proceedings, I thought. "This has just come out and you got to be teaching this to your kids," said Mike. Liking them as much as I did and watching the thirty pairs of eyes now wide with amusement, I hesitated, then stammered, "Well, OK, what's the book, Mike?"

It was Rachel Carson's *Silent Spring*.

On the Green Chain

In the Bomlitz Chemical Company's private forest in Lower Saxony, nothing went to waste. Windfalls were peeled on site with a schaling iron, needles and bark were swept into piles for anthills, branches were scattered and the whole tree was skidded by tractor to the mill yard where the top was cut for fenceposts. There it took two of us with peevees to roll the logs across the yard to a jack ladder and onto the bits for the slow climb to the mill floor. The sawyer sized up each log and then bolted his four or five vertical rip saws into the chuck to get the best out of the log. Then, the reciprocal saw chuck was activated. The log was clamped onto a sliding bed, inching its way through saws that moved methodically up and down, chunk-chunk, chunk-chunk.

Pulling off this green chain was almost as leisurely as preparing the windfalls in the forest. First I watched the log progress for five minutes through the gang saw. Then, as the slabs fell to the side I slid them down a chute to a lower floor. The rough boards were stacked along the loft for later edge-trimming and the sawdust was swept into a lower floor bin while the sawyer prepared the next log. Yawn. An afternoon could pass just sawing the ten logs from the morning's windfalls. After this furious round of mill floor activity it was my job to deal with the debris. First the slabs and trims were cut into a combination of firewood and scaffolding timber. The firewood was sold on the spot as it was cut and the scaffolding timbers were bundled for shipment to Berlin for the construction industry. The sawdust was bagged for mulch and sold almost before it had cooled. At the end of the day, nothing was left but a neat stack of boards and a mill floor suitable for tabling the abendessen.

To get to our job on time each morning, Dave and I purchased an ancient Volkswagen Beetle from a used car dealer in Hannover for five hundred deutsche marks – about C$250 at that time. We rattled out of the lot and got a block or two away before the car lurched to a halt, not to be revived. We fools kicked ourselves as we pushed the VW into a gas station across the road, thinking that our few remaining funds were likely to be entombed there without ceremony. The mechanic gave a brief chuckle, unscrewed the carburetor, hooked the gas line up to the air compressor and blew out the gas line. "Happens all the time with the old ones," he said, and we roared off in relief. For the duration of our ownership of that car, our stops at gas stations included gas for the engine and a blast of compressed air for the gas line.

One day, on the bush part of the job, the tractor driver got his machine high-centered on a six inch stump. Nothing he could do—rocking back and forth, the crew standing around offering advice—would release the machine from its perch. I tried to add to the advice but my limited German fell on deaf ears. Besides, I was just an illiterate guest worker, so how could I know anything? After watching the futile efforts awhile I walked away, cut a length of timber, and used it as a lever. The tractor was off the stump in thirty seconds and I was instantly recognized as the university-trained forestry student that I really was. I had learned that trick getting a panel truck through the mud on the road from Horsefly to Horsefly Bay on Quesnel Lake in 1959—but that is another story.

The bush work was the highlight of our life as forest workers. The day began at first light with us trooping into the forest block, looking for windfalls or other trees that the foreman thought were ready for the mill. The morning passed quickly, broken by a break for coffee and goodies from the local delicatessen: gekochten schinken and edamer kase on pumpernickel. At noon, the crew, mostly ex-army infantry speaking a low German dialect with a very scatological vocabulary (in which they were training us, with disastrous later results in polite society) plopped down to wait for lunch delivery. A unimog ground its way toward us, delivering stacked lunch pails containing soup, sausage with sauerkraut and potatoes, fruit and sucherkuchen and, on Fridays, a bottle of beer.

The lunch was quickly wolfed down to permit us to snooze under a tree for a portion of the hour. Dave was particularly good at this, sometimes getting the foreman exercised with this particular talent. One day nemesis struck in the form of a wandering insect that bit Dave on the lip while he slept. When he awoke to go back to work his upper lip had already achieved twice its normal dimensions. By quitting time it was three times larger. By the time he met his blind date, a comely but unfortunate and horribly shocked flaxen-haired maiden name Hannelore, for an evening at the Hannover Opera, his lip was at least five times its normal size.

Dave, erect of posture, dressed flawlessly in grey flannels, blue blazer and old school tie, a perfect gentleman when seen from behind, resembled in his grotesque disfigurement something more suitable to a showing of beauty and the beast. Despite his careful attention to his date and his impeccable manners, the poor girl was mortified by the spectacle and resolved never to blind date again as long as she lived—and certainly not to see Dave ever again, a promise she kept. My date, who had arranged the outing, never heard from her again either. I often wonder about Hannelore's version of this tale and what she is telling her grandchildren today.

Bush work in Germany, like anywhere else in the world, is a mixture of sweat, swearing and tall tales. Our foreman was a six-foot-six, fair-haired, blue-eyed ex-SS trooper of the elite infantry, not the Gestapo. One day he told Dave and me about his experiences, at our age, fighting the Allied forces in the Battle of the Bulge in the Ardennes forests, near the end of the war.

He spoke about the bravery and determination of his fellow soldiers as the fighting drew near the fatherland. His unit fought the Britons, Americans and Canadians in different battles. His parting line is with me still:

"We only feared to fight the Canadians," he said. As we began to contemplate that thought with some pride, he continued, "They didn't take any prisoners!"

By the Merest Thread

Fritz Fahrenholtz made a fateful decision in Meadow Creek. An old boat performed its last act on the shore of Trout Lake. Two men, who are alive today, were only minutes away from certain death.

Mike Halleran intended to save the Gerrard rainbow trout and I wanted to help him do it. Mike, his cameraman and I were filming the Gerrard rainbow spawning beds downstream from the Trout Lake bridge. Highways had announced that they were going to replace the bridge with a larger structure and it was feared that this would fill the crucial two hundred yards of the Lardeau River gravel with a load of silt. The rainbow trout that spawned in that short reach were the source of one of the largest members of the species, the renowned trophy fish of Kootenay Lake. The film was being shot to air on CBC where Mike was a producer of well-respected, environmentally-oriented shows. We had taken our film and commentary and were sipping coffee in front of the fire in the caretaker's shack, warming happily from the raw March cold outside.

A young RCMP officer and his friend, an insurance adjuster from Trail, had decided to spend the day fishing on Trout Lake. While we were roasting in the cabin, they launched their home-built canoe and paddled out several hundred feet to set their lines. The canoe was unstable and a sudden move threw them both into the frigid water. The officer's identification and sidearm went to the bottom. There was no getting back in the canoe. They attempted to right it by shaking out the water, but it merely rolled like a log. Fifteen or twenty minutes went by as they shouted for help, but there was no one there to hear, no shot they could fire to signal their plight. Their cries did not penetrate the cabin where we sat chatting about saving rainbow trout. They were set to drown as the cold set in and they grew weaker. Shore was much too far away and they feared to let go of the canoe to attempt the swim.

Fritz, of Kootenay Tractor Supply, was making a business call in Meadow Creek that day. As he stepped out the door of the Meadow Creek gas station he looked at the sky and mused: should he make the run back to Nelson right away, or did he have time for a bit of a side trip? It was sunny and the road up the Lardeau is beautiful, so he decided to run up to Trout Lake, take a look around and then go back. He ambled, for there was no hurry, and it must have been while he dawdled along the river that the two men rolled into the water. Fritz arrived at the shore of the lake, stepping out of his car for a breath of fresh mountain air before turning back. He had not heard the men's cries in the car, but now he did. What to do? No boat. Cars at the cabin. Run.

Fritz burst into the cabin with the breathless news that two men were drowning in the lake. We all ran to the shore and stood in a helpless line, listening to the cries grow fainter. Each of us was retreating into the thought of watching two men drown beyond our reach when the caretaker shouted, "I know where there's a boat!" An old, derelict flat-bottom rowboat was leaning up against the back of the cabin. We ran for it. It was made out of plywood that had been solid many years ago. Now, when we grabbed it to carry to the shore, pieces broke easily from the gunwales and left a handful of rotten shavings. Get it to the shore we did, though, with two shiplap boards for paddles.

Mike jumped spontaneously into the boat with his cameraman and prepared to put off—but suddenly hesitated, shouting, "Hey, I can't swim." "I can," I said, and replaced him in the boat.

The cameraman and I paddled the crumbling rowboat out to the two men, now nearly numb with hypothermia and barely treading water. There was no way that we could get both of them in the boat and still be floating—this could quickly turn into four drownings. I tried to shake water out of the canoe so we would have a second boat, but it just rolled and rolled and had to be abandoned. We heaved the insurance adjuster into the rowboat and made him lie on the floorboards. Not much freeboard was left and leaks were beginning to show badly. We tied the RCMP officer on the transom with his belt and began to paddle. It took a long, long time to reach shore. Each minute stretched as we watched for the boat to finally crumble from the strain of paddling with three people's weight and a man dragging behind. We made it, but that was the boat's last trip.

Two violently shivering men were hustled into the cabin. Tea was poured and blankets applied. It took two hours in front of the stove to bring the two men back to a semblance of life. Finally, embarrassed, more than a bit disoriented, and maybe even thankful, they got into their truck and headed back to Trail. The rescuers packed up and headed for homes in Meadow Creek and Nelson. The *Nelson News* ran the story with pictures. Fritz was an agent of fate. Those two lives hung by the merest thread, saved by Fritz's love of the Kootenay back country and a spur-of-the-moment decision to enjoy the day.

Mike's family, Fritz's family and mine all remember this event as defining legend. We have never heard from either of the two men.

ii *influences*

In 1968 I accepted a job offer from Selkirk College to teach botany and ecology. The Community College movement was in full swing and it was the perfect combination of science and teaching so I accepted right away and never looked back. I could not imagine living in the fumes of the Celgar pulp mill, so I trundled up the Kootenay River, looking for clean air. As I drove past the Cora Lynn Dam, rounding the rock bluff, I looked up at the hills above the river and wondered how anyone could place houses so high on the mountains. Over the Taghum bridge, up the hill and down Granite Road, Nelson emerged amid the blossoms of May. It was love at first sight. I bought the first house we looked at from Nick and Nellie Sapriken. It had no siding and the front door emptied into ten feet of space. It was in Blewett, right where those alpine houses had first caught my eye. When we returned to the coast to prepare for the move, a *Nelson News* article had preceded us. There in the press was a picture of the black bear that had tried to claw his way into our newly purchased house, after some of Nellie's newly baked bread. For years, we entertained guests on their dangerous visits to the edge of the wilderness with the claw marks in our screen door.

Nelson was easy to fall in love with. It was its location on the banks of Kootenay Lake where the river begins. It was Baker Street, where you were certain to meet friends within a block or two. It was the social richness, the heritage buildings, the arts, the music, the Doukhobor neighbours, the Americans evading the horror of the Vietnam war, and the family history. Erland Godfrey Hadow, my maternal grandfather, killed on the Somme in the first war, was a land and mine surveyor in Revelstoke in the early years of the twentieth century. Mount Hadow, above Trout Lake, commemorates his love of these Selkirk Mountains. My stepfather, Art Peel, was born in Mirror Lake. My godmother, Mary Gumbert, lived for many years in Nelson—my mother visited the Gumberts on one of the last runs of the Kettle Valley Railway.

Nelson-lovers were assembling in those days of the late sixties. Rod Maennling had taken the Boy Scout Executive Post, Bruce Hunter was a music teacher at LV Rogers High School, Sandy McElroy was a photographer for the *Nelson Daily News* and I was an insufferable crusading ecologist. Somehow our lives connected and a legend was born. One day in 1978, Rod invited Sandy and me, once again living at the coast, to join him on his small sailboat for a spring weekend on Kootenay Lake. When we arrived he said apologetically, "I also invited Bruce Hunter, I hope you don't mind." The four of us bonded permanently over libations in Pilot Bay, vowed to sail again the next year, did so, vowed to do it twice a year, did so, and have recently completed our sixtieth trip together. At trip twenty-six we added to the crew Ed Sutherland, a man with history in New Denver.

As we grew longer in the tooth, discussions of last orders were broached alongside the confidences and exaggerations of our normal conversation. On one occasion Ed brought a bottle of Scotch that his father had given him on his twenty-first birthday, unbelievably still sealed. Sandy quietly took this to heart and created a wooden box capable of holding five bottles of Scotch. Each carefully selected bottle provided by a crew member was to be consumed by the remaining members to celebrate his passing. The unintended consequence is that the likely end of the last two members will be alcohol poisoning or falling off the boat.

Ring and Tone

The Barons sat around the long table, grim-faced, arguing about the fate of the absent King...no, we are not in Runnymede in 1215, but the Selkirk College boardroom in 1970. The Principal had just suspended a member of faculty for unspecified wrongdoing. The problem was that the person in question was a man of colour, and thus his incensed colleagues and some of the department chairmen were interpreting the situation as a case of racial discrimination, while others had not yet leapt to any conclusions. Voices were raised, dudgeon was high—there were those that would have the Principal dismissed for an act of great social repugnance. "Off with his head!" was the sentiment.

The Chairman of the Aviation Department rose to the Principal's defence, attesting that he knew the validity of the case but could not speak to the details. This did not satisfy the righteous indignation of the defenders of human rights, and the debate raged. Some of us represented a cooler contingent and argued that we should not rush to judgment, knowing nothing of the issues that motivated the Principal in his action. As the arguments showed no signs of resolution, I was deputized to call the Principal to seek his explanation. "Hi Andy, we're gathered in the boardroom at the moment, the Chairmen are deeply concerned by the suspension—can you give us the reason for your action?" "No, Bruce, I cannot. The matter is under investigation, but it is serious, and you will just have to trust me." "Some Chairmen believe that you are in the wrong, Andy." "I can understand how they feel, Bruce. They will just have to trust me in this. If they can't bring themselves to do that, then I will resign!" I delivered this conversation to the assembled Chairmen and the table voted, by a majority, not a consensus, that the Principal was to be trusted but that an explanation was needed as soon as possible.

Slowly the story came to light. It happened that aviation students had begun to find pornographic pictures inserted into the books recommended for reading in their reference section of the library. One particularly prominent picture was of an erect member held by a well-employed hand; an eight-by-fourteen masterpiece, so to speak. Unfortunately for the picture's subject, he was incontrovertibly identifiable. The pigmentation aside, the large, distinct, and well-known signet ring could belong to none other than our suspended colleague. It was not a case of discrimination but one of shameless display and certain identity.

After the manic laughter subsided, and the reverberating chuckles finally died down (some continued many years later), there were one or two Barons that were sorely disappointed in being diverted from the satisfying spectacle of impeaching the King. In the great scheme of things, justice prevailed. The Orb and the Sceptre were saved by the Tone and the Ring.

Long live the King!

Battlefield Promotion

I taught ecology, botany, biology, forestry and regional planning, became a department chairman, made Selkirk College my life, and came to see the Principal's job as a career target. When the position became available, I applied and lost to a more senior man—no sweat, he came from a fabled California Community College and had ten years on me! I found out the results of the competition from a note in my mailbox addressed to "All Faculty," not through any direct courtesy that a runner-up and internal candidate might expect.

It did not take the new broom many months to run afoul of the department head barons. Selkirk management consisted of a Principal, a Bursar, a Dean of Students, a Dean of Studies and a group of department chairmen. The Principal presided over the institution, using the chairmen as a sounding board, and consulted them regularly on the decisions of the day. It was a simple system, deftly managed, and served the college well. The new man decided that the divisional management structure he remembered from California, and a much larger institution, would be better—and of course he would eliminate the old cabal of Barons who seemed to have too much power and too much love for history.

Unfortunately, though he was clearly well-meaning, he misread the Selkirk culture and the solidarity of the Chairmen and confidence began to slide. Abandoning the divisional idea because of so much disagreement, and desperately searching for a bacon-saving strategy, he next tried to institute a College Forum that would involve absolutely everyone in large group advice-making, according himself with the prerogative of vetoing any uncomfortable advice that might emerge. Again, he underestimated those troublesome Barons and the slide became an avalanche. As things wore on, Selkirk entered a budget period in which the Ministry of Education began making threatening noises about cutting back the college budget because our cost per student was way above the provincial average. Our fearless leader mistook the intimidation coming from the ministry as the gospel truth and made plans for program reductions and faculty layoffs. Selkirk was just taking off as a community college—guess how that news was received by the Barons!

The Barons revolted and made complaints to the College Council; I prepared a "Blueprint for Survival," mimeographed copies on alcohol spirit masters (I didn't have time to do a Gestetner master and Xerox had not been invented yet), and nailed the thesis to the cathedral door. All hell broke loose. The Council stepped into the fray. On a Thursday night they fired the Principal and also the Dean of Studies, who had unwisely sided with the divisional idea. The Council then asked the Barons to submit three names of department chairmen in whom they had confidence to take over as Acting Principal. The Barons put forward me and two others on Friday, the Council selected me on Saturday and on a Monday morning in 1972 I was in the head office at thirty-two years of age—the youngest CEO in the College system.

I quickly became restless as Acting Principal, taking the burden of leadership without the mandate, so I held a referendum among the faculty asking whether the Council should appoint me as full Principal or put the job up for recruitment.

I got a 74 percent majority vote, the Council appointed me and I became the only college Principal in Canada elected to office by the faculty of the institution.

Appeal Court

One of my tasks as Principal of Selkirk College was to adjudicate appeals from students who had been suspended or dismissed by the faculty of a department. The worst cases always came from either the nurses or the aviators. They both used the same damning phrase to eliminate a student that deviated from their preferred norms. "They are not safe in the ward!" "They are not safe in the cockpit!" So how on earth could a plant ecologist, having descended to the indecent trade of administrator, adjudicate an issue of life or death, invoked by trained professionals? The rules demanded that I do so, that's how!

On one such occasion, I was faced with a young man who had been dismissed by the Aviation Department. His file came with the expected label: unsafe in the cockpit. I was immediately suspicious of this terminal accusation—it seemed so watertight and conclusive, a judgment that could follow a young man forever on his academic record. Was it justified? The young men taking the aviation course were highly select and their families were paying enormous sums for their training. Graduates were targeted to major airlines and a most prestigious career. To be dismissed from the course was the summary execution of a life dream.

What did the record say? He was an average student according to his academic grades. He had successfully acquired his private pilot's licence, flying the small planes allotted to the students of the program from a commercial Castlegar flight school. The faculty caught him falsifying his log book, recording flight hours that did not take place. It was the dishonesty that sank him. An airline pilot, responsible for the lives of many, who falsified his records could not be tolerated. Suspension upheld!

The Fate of Judges

Some months later, as part of the College's extension service to the East Kootenays, I was preparing for a flight to Cranbrook with a member of the mathematics department. It was a fine, clear day and we were standing on the tarmac by the plane, a twin-engined Piper Cherokee, waiting for the pilot to complete his flight plan. As we stood chatting, a woman charged out of the airport building with two children in tow. She was clearly agitated. As she got near I could hear that she was shrieking at me. "You are completely irresponsible to be subjecting my husband to such danger! Don't you see that this flight is putting our family at risk? He could die and leave me destitute and his two children fatherless! How could you be such a heartless monster?"

I was slightly taken aback, not just by her demeanor and her accusations, but by the fact that her husband, the mathematician, stood silent during the harangue, looking calmly over the runway in the direction of our intended flight. While I was trying to explain that it was a clear day, that we were flying in a twin-engined plane, and that the trip was less than one hour, all the while being savaged by his wife, he tuned out and gave me no help at all. I began to suspect that this was not the first such experience and that facing death by plane crash might not be all that bad. I was finally saved from this impossible situation when the pilot walked briskly onto the tarmac, jumped into the plane and exhorted us to follow.

The pilot was the student I had suspended those few months before. He was now a private charter pilot in Castlegar for the firm that trained the aviation students. It was my knuckles that were white as we flew for one hour, twin engines humming flawlessly, in a cloudless sky, over the Purcell Range to Cranbrook, the mathematician still imperturbable and unaware of his potential for deliverance.

Two Nights Before Christmas

I had discovered Errazuriz. Here was a Chilean red wine that was better than most and priced to keep us wage earners launching our end-of-day conversations in the tradition of the landed gentry. Uncork, breathe, decant, fill the cheese tray and sit back with philosophical intent. The trip to the grog shop after work was just a small diversion from the traffic wars. Turn, park, shop and race for the highway. But today was different.

Outside the liquor store I often had to run the gauntlet of buskers and panhandlers, and in this season also the plastic bubble with the jingle bells—well situated in the action zone frequented by the partners Indulgence and Guilt. Occasionally a coin or two would pass across the divide, always leaving a feeling of uneasy inadequacy in their wake. It is hard to submerge the mixed feelings of contempt and sympathy on any day of the year—if you are still employed—but at Christmas these feelings are much more complicated. There is a heightened sense of the losses: the absence of family, the resort to life at the bottom, trading dignity for spare change at a time that emphasizes generosity of spirit and largesse.

Of course, the intellectual feat is to sort the unprincipled from the needy, the professionals from the cast-downs, the charlatans from the truly down and out. There is always the suspicion that you are being played the fool by the man with a BMW parked around the corner. You know, the one with the penthouse suite in the city who leaves his crutches in the trunk of the car at the end of a profitable day on the street. He too cracks an Errazuriz to usher in the evening.

Well, today was different.

As I threaded my way into the shuffle at the store entrance, a woman thrust herself into my consciousness. She was more urgent, aggressive even, but at the same time deeply embarrassed, and her voice had the shrillness of desperation. There was something more here that stuck with me at the Errazuriz display. Leaving the store with the bag of clanking bottles, I fished out a twenty-dollar bill to pass along—it was a measure of my elevated unease that I felt a few coins would not quite do. I stopped to talk to her, something I would not normally think of doing; after all this was a city and I didn't know her or anyone else around. I asked her story.

Her embarrassment was real, not feigned for the occasion. "I was laid off three weeks ago, there is no food in the house, I can't make my rent, I don't have anything for my son, I'm a single mom and I don't know what to do—I'm sorry!" She had been a twelve-dollar-an-hour worker at the Sunset Lodge (run by the Salvation Army) with nothing to spare for savings, living in the hand-to-mouth world of the working poor, the people we have turfed out of the safety net, outsourcing their menial jobs to ensure that the rest of us can afford our Errazuriz. I gave her the twenty dollars, she gave me a hug—she smelled of clean clothes—I wished her well and stumbled to the car feeling that I had not done what the occasion truly called for. The next day I went back with a month's rent in a roll of bills but she was gone. I have never seen her again. She haunts me.

Just in Time

In 1975, as oil prices soared and world famine was predicted, having a year's supply of food in the house was a Boy Scout's dream. Freeze-dried oatmeal packed in nitrogen, buckets of wheat, tubs of honey and boxes of salt. Extra axe handles and a barrel of kerosene stored in the shed. Oh yes, and the trade goods. Small bottles of brandy, jars of instant coffee and cans of cigarette tobacco lined the secret shelf in the cold room. A small stock of gold coins in a money belt completed the hoard. In the closet a 30:30 Winchester and plenty of ammunition. Let the collapse begin!

That year I had a group of summer students look into how much food we had in the Kootenays in case things went wrong. They investigated the three firms that had food warehouses in Trail and Nelson and interviewed the managers of Safeway and Super Value stores. They talked to the trucking firms. What they found was profoundly disturbing.

The West Kootenays had two weeks' supply of food in the local warehouses, most of it canned and packaged and half of which was pet food! All the rest of our supermarket supply, all the fresh goods, came in a constant flow by truck. What would happen if the Safeway trucks stopped rolling? This thought fed the preparatory urge because we knew that the stores shelves would empty in a single day if disaster struck.

Of course the Mormon families had their year's supply and our Doukhobor neighbours had always stored their winter supply of food. The majority of us citified folk would perish but not without a fight for the stored supplies of the well prepared.

Now, a generation later, there are no warehouses of food in the West Kootenays. There are very few warehouses anywhere. We are now in the era of just-in-time everything. Manufacture to order, grow, pick and ship. There is no wasted investment in expensive, depreciating stock. Bring it in from Mexico or California the next day by air freight. Slaughter, butcher, pack and ship. The Safeway trucks are at the store every day. Shelf-stocking is constant. Beef from Alberta, apples from New Zealand, prawns from Thailand and oranges from Israel are always there. We live in the modern world of flow. We shop nearly every day. We eat what is pre-packaged. Our kitchens have no pantry. Our houses lack a cold room and architects don't plan root cellars in town houses. We are linked into all parts of the planet for our food and we need it to be available right now.

The air, like in 1975, is full of dire predictions. When, not if, the bird flu pandemic strikes, they say, we will face extensive disruption of our just-in-time systems as the operators fall by the wayside or refuse to expose themselves to contagion. Hospitals will overflow, schools will close, offices will be dark. The supermarkets will be stripped in moments. Who will maintain the chlorinated water supply? Who will stock the shelves if the farmers in Mexico are decimated by the flu? What if they close the borders to prevent infectious people from traveling? How much produce do we make in those Fraser Valley greenhouses anyway?

Is it time to stock the basement, load the 30:30, order more bottled water? Or will these predictions prove, once again, too apocalyptic to be true, sparing us for our next growth curve in our just-in-time world? When do we reach the threshold? And will we be prepared?

The Blewett Watershed

One day in 1975 the rumour flew: they were going to log our watershed—my watershed!—on the slopes of Blewett, south of Nelson. Vera Soukerukoff, philosopher queen, gas jockey and legendary borscht maker, intercepted the rumour and insisted that she knew some substantial women who would make those bulldozer drivers think twice! She told everyone who traded at her gas station at the corner of Granite and Blewett Roads—and that was a lot of people.

We had the largest public meeting ever held at the Blewett School and let Crestbrook Forest Industries and the Forest Service know that this was not business as usual. We formed the Blewett Watershed Committee and got into the environmental-activist mode, confronting the government and company foresters with a united front of public opposition. Feelings ran high about water in this area because our domestic and irrigation supply was based on water licenses on surface creeks that ran down from the steep mountain slopes behind our houses. Most of us had individual intakes and some were rudimentary group efforts, but none had any kind of filtration or treatment. We could easily envision what the logging practices common in the West Kootenays of the 1970s would do to those creeks.

For a while we were either ignored or stonewalled—this was the seventies, after all. Meanwhile, a dispute between two Blewett neighbours over a shared water line was settled abruptly when one shot the other in the leg with a .22 rifle. Though it had nothing to do with the Watershed Committee, it got the undivided attention of the local foresters! (I'm reasonably sure they believed us that it was not just a brilliant negotiating tactic.) In time, as the broad-based committee of citizens solidified, we began to take a positive negotiation approach. "We do not oppose logging of the crown land above our houses," we said. "It is not our land or our right to prevent its use, but we have high standards for the operations and many concerns about the hauling of logs on Blewett's narrow roads." We wanted exceptional harvesting and road building practices, we did not want huge clear cuts and we did not want loaded logging trucks forcing school buses into the ditch!

All of this building tension came together in an historic meeting in the planning department's offices in the Forest Service Regional Office in Nelson. It was a classic: Blewett Watershed Committee members on one side of the table, company officials on the other, and stressed government foresters at each end. Was this to be fireworks or settlement?

John Cuthbert, who was later to become the province's Chief Forester, was the government forester in charge. With great courage in the face of what could have become an angry standoff, he said to the company representatives, "I will not issue you a single cutting permit until you have come to an accommodation with the watershed committee!" Two minutes of stunned silence ensued, dawning horror on one side of the table and dawning jubilation on the other.

To his great credit, John Murray, Crestbrook's Chief Forester, rose to the occasion. He rallied his troops and began the process of earning the community's trust and respect, taking each of the Watershed Committee's concerns and systematically addressing them. The first thing he solved was the road issue. He negotiated the use of the Kootenay Canal Road for hauling logs, a road that had until then been closed to public traffic, thus resolving that potentially show-stopping conflict. He then hired Greg Lay, a respected local forester, to lay out the roads and cut blocks in consultation with the committee. Further, he sited in the community a young company forester, Joe Tress, as a resident, and instructed him to work closely with water users on a daily basis.

The cut blocks were small, the visible impact was minor, the roads were well engineered, the stream crossings were well sited and constructed, and the water flowed clean most of the time. One morning, Joe phoned one of our members with the warning, "Close off your system, we had a culvert blowout and there is mud in the water!" The valves were closed, the systems remained clean, the mud passed through and the culvert was repaired the same day. That was trust-building in action. The collaborative working arrangement built by the company and the watershed committee is still operating thirty years later—the longest running arrangement of this kind in the province. The constructive approach by both sides became a model for public involvement in forestry. As a result, I was asked to train Forest Service personnel in public involvement at the forest service training school at Green Timbers in Surrey, a few yards from where, at age nineteen, I had lurched into gear with that marvelous Land Rover.

A generation of personnel went through those courses. John Cuthbert has since retired as Chief Forester but his legacy remains.

Crusader

Vladimir Krajina could deliver a three-hour lecture without a break. There was, however, on most occasions, a long digression or two. In the midst of explaining how climate, organisms and geology could give rise to ecosystems, he would launch into a discussion of western democracy or the evils of slashburning, or the ghost-town future of Vancouver that would result from shoddy forestry, and return fifteen minutes later to his exact point of departure. Most of my fellow students had checked out by then, but I always followed him round the circles of his mind.

One such digression began even before the lecture. Our group of ecology students was chatting in the classroom, waiting for Vladimir to appear. He strode into the room in his usual fashion, a stack of papers under his arm, but he appeared unusually severe. He paused. It was November 22, 1963. "President Kennedy has just been shot," he said. His lecture that day was not about ecology at all, but about the wages of democracy and the necessity of its constant defence.

Vladimir was a passionate crusader. While he lectured at exhaustive length on the bio-geo-climatic ecology of the province, he was as likely to deliver himself of a caution on the necessary defense of democracy. Vladimir was trained by Professor Domin at Prague University to be exceptionally thorough as a botanist and ecologist, but his academic career was only one part of his life.

For the brief but heady time in Czech history between occupation by the Nazis and domination by the Communists, Vladimir Krajina was Secretary of State in the democratic government of Jan Marsaryk. When Marsaryk was murdered, "falling" to his death from a hotel window like the journalists of contemporary Russia, the government dissolved and Vladimir fled in the night to Britain as the guest of Churchill. From there he applied to universities worldwide that might take him as a botanist. By sheer luck it was the University of British Columbia that offered him a post.

What Vladimir brought to our province was more than his formal talent as a scientist. He also brought his passion as a democrat—a passion that was sorely tested and fire-hardened. Thus when he expostulated to our class of forestry students on the necessary stewardship of the institutions of democracy, we listened with the kind of attention only paid to true experience. For me, ecology and democracy are inextricably linked by his example—a conjunction that has influenced me for a professional lifetime.

By 1980, I had obtained a doctorate as his student, taught ecology to forestry technologists at Selkirk College, served the institution as president and was working as a senior public servant in the Community College division of the Ministry of Education. Restless in the educational bureaucracy, I was invited by Mike Apsey, Bill Young and Carl Highsted to a seconded post in the Ministry of Forests, where I established their public involvement policy and program. It was an opportunity to combine a formal education in ecology with the practice of democracy.

So Vladimir's legacy was materializing in hybrid form as public engagement in forest management—the application of democracy at the practical day-to-day level, where the electoral system was supplemented by access to the machinery of government. It was my job to invent the process by which ordinary people could influence what was done in their forests, their watersheds, their wilderness, their wildlife habitats and their landscapes. My conviction was that a truly effective democracy is rich in the public institutions of education and resource management and, through them, actively engaged in the stewardship of both environment and society.

This philosophy was woven into a planning system manual and into a ministry policy to govern public participation in forestry planning throughout the province. My program included training in public participation methods for agency staff and resulted in a series of advisory committees in areas of controversy. Public planning groups concerned with community watersheds were begun in Creston and Kelowna; on Meares Island and the Queen Charlottes, groups concerned with wilderness conservation and the rights of First Nations formed. It was the beginning of the multi-stakeholder planning processes now so familiar in British Columbia.

The statement on the function of public engagement in a democracy that appeared in the participatory methods manual was written at the Oak Bay Marina and later became the Ministry of Forests *Public Involvement Handbook*. It was handwritten in the summer sun that was beating down on the cockpit of my twenty-six-foot Haida sailboat, appropriately named *Crusader*.

Landing or Not

The sailing couple had no idea what awaited them at the head of Kootenay Lake. It was a long, slow trip in their twenty-two-foot sloop from Woodbury Creek and they were unfamiliar with the anchorages.

Meanwhile, a pair of Frasers and a slip of a wood nymph were whiling away a brilliant afternoon on the wharf at Johnson's Landing. Kootenay Lake, as always, was just above freezing and made for a very bracing swim. The three of us had dipped in the lake, briefly of course, and were sun-drying in a little shivering threesome. As we slowly regained normal temperatures, a small sailboat hove into view. It took a long while before we could see that it was crewed by a middle-aged couple, the wife standing on the bow, boat hook in hand, preparing to tie up to the Johnson's Landing wharf where we were sitting.

Picture the scene: three naked people on the wharf, two comely women and one somewhat less comely male. Naked. The boat approached inexorably with the husband at the tiller, engine roaring, shouting tie-up instructions to his mate. She couldn't clearly hear her tillerman, nor could she make herself clear to him. It slowly began to dawn on the mate with the boathook that something was amiss on the Johnson's Landing wharf. At first she made a small incredulous bleat: "Those people are *naked*." She turned to her husband and made a discreet waving-off motion, suggesting that he turn away from the wharf. He ignored her, of course, not hearing the diminutive bleat and not anxious to forego a safe landing spot.

By then she was seriously agitated. "Those *people* are *naked*!" she shouted, but to no avail. The boat simply glided closer. "THOSE PEOPLE ARE NAKED," she shrieked to her husband, who still did not understand the source of the incredible dance being performed on the bow of the boat. Why didn't she just get on with preparing to tie up? Meanwhile, the three naked people, two Frasers and a wood nymph, were drying comfortably and getting increasingly amused. Sound carries well across water. We almost stood up to wave them into the wharf.

Finally, with one horrific explosion of angst, the lookout, averting her eyes away from the offending scene, confronted her husband with waving arms and pointing fingers and the ultimate volume she could command. "THOSE PEOPLE ARE NAKED!" At this point we began to suspect that her husband had been in the know from the very beginning, and had been ignoring the warning in order to get a closer look. We couldn't see any binoculars, but what captain would be without them in unknown waters? They drew close enough for us to see the whites of their eyes, the husband's being particularly visible.

With great reluctance he finally turned the boat to steam on by, looking for an anchorage without offending Frasers and wood nymphs. Later that evening, we suspect, he was still trying to explain why he did not hear her warning cries until he was close enough to see for himself. The reputation of Johnson's Landing remains intact.

The Waters Close

One thing I have learned in higher office: the waters close in moments over your tenure, and your legacy, if any, is quickly appropriated by the new regime, without attribution and with only brief ceremonial passage. Thus it was at Selkirk College, the Ministry of Education, and Malaspina College. It will be the same at the Forest Practices Board. The King is Dead, Long Live the King!

At Selkirk, as its Principal, I steered the College through a recession, an attempt to amalgamate with Notre Dame University, a doubling of the faculty and the establishment of remote services in outlying communities. It was a wild ride during the development heydays of the community college movement in BC. But, when the College held its forty-year anniversary in 2006, no one thought to invite me to the occasion. The current President is content with the present.

As Executive Director of Post Secondary Education Programs in the Ministry of Education in the late seventies, I developed the program approval system; established a program department; fostered programs ranging from mining to computers; approved the program justifications for expanding Douglas College among others; acted as the ministry delegate to the Board of the Open Learning Institute; helped to promulgate the new college and institute legislation; and wrote the legislation for the Justice Institute. I have never heard from any ministry officials in the thirty years since.

As President of Malaspina College I helped steer the institution through the 1980s recession; expand the programs and budget while others were laying off teachers; build a campus in Powell River and save one in Parksville; build a training restaurant; get the province to allow foreign students in community colleges for the first time; enroll Japanese and Chinese students; and earn 50 percent of the entire contract income gained by the twenty-two colleges and institutes of the province in a single year. In 2007, at the installation of the fifth President (to which I was belatedly invited), I sat anonymous in the halls that I had helped to build, silent, holding history in my mind and heart, but merely a decorative fixture in a ceremony devoid of the nuances of even the most recent past.

At the Forest Practices Board, as Chair, I promoted a concern for the whole environment, with management of place as the basis of sustaining the ecosystems of the province. I gave credit to industrial foresters where it was due, fostered the development of explicit criteria for forestry performance, and challenged the slide toward private control of the commons. When I left in 2010, I expected the same quick oblivion—my six-year stint to be shredded among the redundant files, as the electronic blizzard of minutiae overcomes history and the new incumbent.

So what is the legacy of a professional lifetime? It is the ecology students I influenced at Selkirk who are now senior managers, the young people who got access to an education from the new programs developed during ministry days, the students taught by teachers at Malaspina who weren't laid off in the eighties recession and the thirty-somethings who were inspired by a vision of a different land ethic that honored commitment to place above the pursuit of commodity markets organized on behalf of the rich.

Yes, the only thing that outlasts a tenure is the influence on people—not the artifacts, the buildings, the strategy documents, but the chances given to people and the respect for the planet that might have been instilled in a receptive few. With that I am content, though there are moments when a little adulation from the powers that be go a long way.

On one such occasion, an evening in 2007, I attended a night of recognition for public service in British Columbia, at which two of our board staff were being honoured. The scene was Government House in Victoria, with the new First Nation Lieutenant Governor officiating. I read the lists, sipping a glass of wine and chatting with Sarah, my colleagues and their partners. On the lists were two of my Selkirk forestry students, one being recognized for thirty-five years and the second for a full forty years of service. We met and stories were shared. They both recalled their student days with affection. I rest my case.

iii *adventures*

My last year as President of Malaspina College was a tumultuous one. Our broadly representative council had been turned by statute from a champion of community college development into a politically-appointed fiscal watchdog for the government. It was the recession of the 1980s and sails were being trimmed under a strong blast of wind from right field. I fought back and they got me—an operating deficit in the financing of the World Conference on Youth Employment, the most widely inclusive such gathering on the planet to that time, was used as a pretext to get rid of the outspoken president. I was thunderstruck by the way it was conducted, political intrigue in full flower, and by the fact that it effectively ended my formal career in education. Well, it ended my employment for one full day. Simon Fraser University drafted me into a team working on a CIDA-sponsored science curriculum at Indonesia's eastern islands universities. I signed my severance papers in Vancouver Airport and flew to Jakarta. I spent seventeen years consulting in Africa, Asia, the Middle East and the Caribbean before I joined the Forest Practices Board—a steady job, with predictable holidays and weekends off.

Attack of the Fungi

Snorkeling on Bunaken Reef offshore Manado, the Christian city on the northern tip of Sulawesi in Indonesia, had consequences. At first, we floated in a foot or two of crystal-clear water, hovering over a kaleidoscope of corals and multicoloured fish. The eye was saturated with the blues and yellows of striped fish, the greens and mauves of sponges, filigreed tentacles of feeding corals and the darting of fluorescent minnows. Eventually, the gentle current took us over the edge of the reef, and suddenly we were looking down through dark blue-green water until it eventually becomes black. In an instant the fascination of the reef turned to sphincter-tightening fear of the deep. I felt like a tidbit of shark bait and flailed my way to the reef boat, hoisting my way up the rope ladder as fast as I could without sparking the laughter of my Indonesian guides. It's impossible to be nonchalant looking down into that dark mystery.

I didn't become a meal for something lurking below the edge of the reef—it was something else that got me.

When the trip was over and all the pale white men were back aboard the reef boat, with its open well in the centre, we turned for the hour-long ride back to Manado. There were no towels or clothes, just the bathing suits we were wearing and the canopy overhead to prevent being fried by the equatorial sun. We were warm, moist and susceptible. This was the perfect environment for the fungi awaiting newly-exposed North American flesh. Certainly they were waiting for mine.

About a day later I noticed a splotch of reddish grey on the inside of my right thigh. Within hours it grew into the most virulent looking crotch rot that I had ever seen. Now it was mottled, itchy and aggressive. It was too embarrassing to mention for a day or two, until it went from itch to agony. As it was also perilously close to consuming my male identity, I eventually mentioned my condition to the party manager, who was fortunately an old hand in Indonesia and a man of unexcitable disposition.

By this time we had flown to the south end of Sulawesi, to the city of Ujung Pandang, where I assumed that there might be medical help. There was, but not in the form I had imagined. My leader assured me that he knew an Indonesian army medical officer of long acquaintance who could fix me up. He would be along to the hotel in an hour. It was a long hour. When the doctor arrived, clad in khaki uniform, the contrast to a sterile medical clinic peopled with staff in white coats gave me more than a slight pause. When he examined my now entirely scrofulous underpinnings his exclamation of surprise—"What on earth have you been doing?"—chilled my spine. I assumed that he was used to treating soldiers who had visited the brothels of Macassar and was labeling me as one of those tourists who had no clue about the consequences. I explained that I had been snorkeling on Bunaken Reef and his raised eyebrows receded slightly.

My eyebrows were the next to be raised as he took from his medical kit a huge stainless steel syringe with a needle that looked like a veterinary tool. "Bend over," he said, with bored medical detachment. I did, but with considerable attachment and the mixed emotions of one receiving a large, not visibly sterilized needle, delivered in a hotel room in the tropics, containing whatever it was. "Cortisone," he later explained, to reduce the skin trauma, and, "Here is a prescription for an anti-fungal cream. Use it liberally until it is all gone." He left in smart military fashion amid my profuse thanks and sublimated trepidation.

Well, the combination eventually worked, but not before the fungus had invaded my armpits, eyelids and eyebrows and I had become a rather grotesque combination of mottling and unguents—which led, I'm sure to the great affection of my fellow travellers.

We spent the last night before the departure of the team to Irian Jaya in a guesthouse in Ambon. We had been diverted there by the shuttle driver, who, having learned where we were booked, insisted that his cousin's hotel was a much better choice. His cousin did not believe in wasting diesel-powered electricity on air conditioning, so the night was both conducive to the remaining fungus and noisy with the sound of insects that would normally have been masked by the conditioner fans. I awoke at first light to find that my fungus-riddled body was now stitched with the tracks of some biting insect, scarlet rail lines carved across my chest. Being consigned to Irian's reputedly lethal forms of malaria seemed like the next logical step in this progression.

On the flight from Ambon to Irian, we touched down on the island of Biak, where MacArthur, on his fabled return, began the march to overcome the Japanese forces occupying Indonesia and the Philippines. The Japanese troops had gone underground in caves when the Americans arrived. The solution to this tactic was to pour gasoline in the cave mouths and light up. At the bottom of one such gloomy cave, now covered in green algae and mosses, stands a small stone obelisk engraved with Japanese characters, remembering the incinerated soldiers.

The hoteliers of Biak had arranged it so the flight schedules for Garuda, Indonesia's airline, did not permit transfer to Irian without an overnight stay. So, on to another cousin's hotel. This time we were wiser and asked to see the rooms in advance. They looked perfectly comfortable and had visible air conditioners, but our most imperturbable professor, without hesitation, whipped off a bed cover to expose the sheets. The bed was covered with a million ants. "No problem," he said, "I'll take this room, I'm an entomologist!" There was no argument from me. My room was without entomological interest and I did not attract any further attention from the fauna of the island.

By the time that we departed for Irian, my corporeal passenger list had subsided and all I had to consider were the various forms of malaria. As it turned out, the trip, but for one experience, was completely benign—we saw the night fishers' lights offshore from the city of Jayapura, we visited with the Melanesian governor of Irian Jaya, we lamented the Javanizaton of the islands with young faculty members, and we devised science curricula for the local university. The chemistry lab at the university, however, may well have been lethal. The chemical storeroom had a full complement of experimental supplies provided by a previous aid project. Fortunately, it appeared most of the glass containers had never been opened. The chemicals had been there for a number of years, stewing in the tropical heat of the unconditioned laboratory: as soon as we entered the door the stench of interacting chemicals was evident. I wondered how many classes of students had been asphyxiated there and whether the explosion would occur while I was in the room. I wrote a rapid cautionary report and headed for the fresh air.

Our supreme project leader was a professor from Simon Fraser University, interested in the intellectual task of determining a science curriculum for the universities of the Eastern Indonesian Islands but uninterested in the potential risks of visiting the remotest areas. We were slated to go from Jayapura to the small town of Manokwari, out on the "head of the bird", the outer reaches of the island of New Guinea, which resembles the bird of paradise in shape. Irian backcountry was reputed to be the home of incurable cerebral malaria, a malady that conveyed a three-day maximum life span for those who contracted it. Our leader decided at that point that he, along with the other professors, should return to Jakarta to begin writing the all-important trip report. This meant that the visit to Manokwari should be conducted by the consultants and the CIDA officers, expendable as we were.

We flew for four hours over untracked rain forest in a single-engine missionary four-seater. As far as the eye could see, the only break in the forest was the occasional tropical river, flowing from the highlands into the sea. That vista is now broken by logging concessions and the world laments the loss of one of its lungs. The research station in Manokwari, the object of our visit, was peopled with young enthusiasts. We were taken by Toyota land cruiser into the experimental plots where crops were being developed and pest controls were being devised. It was the furthest outpost of the Indonesian Empire and it was wonderful.

Jakarta may have been safer, but Manokwari, without terminal cerebral malaria or any new fungi, was much more interesting!

Your Daughter is a Bright Young Girl...

The Chief Constable of Virgin Gorda awoke in the middle of the night to find it much lighter than the hour would suggest. The light was rather orange in hue and it flickered on his bedroom wall. With sudden realization he crashed out of bed, stumbling to the window, to see his police land rover fully engulfed in flames. He could not see anyone, but he knew that he had just been delivered a message. It could have been the house.

The British Virgin Islands, among many such Caribbean nations, is plagued as a transshipment point and money-laundering location for the drug trade. When my West Indian colleague and I were working with the BVI government to review the salary structure of the civil service, I had the privilege of interviewing much of their police force. Young constables earned just enough to keep them in their bachelor barracks, ensuring that they could not get married. Senior officers earned more, but it was a mere pittance compared to the proceeds of drug-running and a scant bulwark against offers or coercion. Remaining honest in such circumstances takes real character, fortunately there in abundance.

On Wednesdays in BVI's capital, Roadtown, on the island of Tortola, two gentlemen would disembark from the ferry from St. John in the US Virgin Islands, carrying two large suitcases each. They used the ferry route because of agreements allowing the traditional movement of Virgin Islanders among the islands that did not require a visit with customs on entry. The men walked the short distance from the ferry landing to a central bank, where, in a back room, they unloaded their four cases of tightly bundled US cash for deposit, roughly one million dollars a case. Every Wednesday. The bank clerk who described this weekly transaction to my consulting colleague mentioned that we might not want to identify him to anyone as a source of this information lest he soon disappear. Our knowledge might also be a bit of a hazard to us, he suggested.

Arson, disappearance and disfigurement are at the crude end of the coercion spectrum. Simple bribery is more common. But more subtle and terrifying methods are also used to protect the trade. The Chief Constable of Virgin Gorda had a twelve-year-old daughter in the local school—a good student, bright and cheerful. When the burning of the police land rover did not have the desired effect on policing, another approach was tried: one day on the street the Chief Constable was casually approached by a man with another message.

"Hey man, you have a lovely daughter. I hear she doin' real well at school. Too bad there no chance for a bright kid to go for higher education in these islans. Hear me, I have a fren' in New York, he workin' for an exclusive girls' school with amazin', record placin' graduates in the best universities. I could arrange for your sweet daughter to go there, all expense paid, man. She could have a wunnerful future.

"On de other hand, my man, your girl leave for school at 7:45 every mornin'. She walk your street to Alvin Vanterpool's corner shop where she buy a sweet. A few minute later, she turn corner down Carpenter's Hill to minibus stop where she wait, alone, five minutes till Frankie's bus come. When she get out de bus at Orlando's petrol, she jus' take she time lookin' in Euphemia's dress shop window, 'fore she join she frens for dat las' block to she school. When she leave she school at 3:05, she retrace mos' of de same step, by sheself for some long, long time at four differen' place.

"Your choice, man!"

The Chief Constable drives his daughter to and from school. Every day.

Fire Drill

Interviewing firemen in the British Virgin Islands is not about sitting down to talk, especially not with the firemen at the Beef Island Airport. They had to show me!

Beef Island is a low-lying piece of land to the north of Tortola, fringed by mangroves and bush and by the clear, blue-green waters of lagoons and channels. It is bridged to Tortola by the thirty-foot steel span of Rube Goldberg Toll Bridge, complete with manned tollbooth and swinging arm, commissioned with due ceremony by Queen Elizabeth herself. The airport could take small planes of twin otter capacity, commuter planes of the American Airlines feeder company, planes of questionable provenance owned by Air BVI, or other cast-offs from more affluent societies to the north. Many landings are by private planes, with pilots and passengers heading to the resorts and yacht charters for which BVI is justly famous.

The fire crew at the airport is autonomous from the fire establishment in Roadtown, Tortola's main town and BVI's capital, some forty minutes' drive away. It is a small crew, but an enthusiastic one. As I was interviewing them about their future salary structure, they were anxious to impress me with their capacity to respond to an air crash. The fire service had one fire truck with chemical-retardant-holding tank and cab-mounted monitor. I was hustled into the cab and fitted with a fireproof coat in which I sweltered in the thirty-degree heat and near-rainfall humidity. We roared out of the covering shed, revved the pump engine and blasted retardant-laced water in a two-hundred-foot arc into the airport bushes. With growing enthusiasm for the demonstration, swiveling the monitor back and forth, we emptied the tank. Retardant dripped from the roof into the cab, entering my bloodstream through the skin. I can still taste it and wonder to this day what that did to my genetic complement and whether rum could effectively flush it out of my system. I certainly tried.

At some point it occurred to the fire crew that we had just emptied the only fire vehicle at the airport and that it might be appropriate to refill it in case it was actually needed, particularly as planes were continuing to land and take off while the demonstration was being conducted. There were no above-ground storage tanks at the island, so the fresh water for the truck's tank was located on the far side of the runway from the garage, in concrete bunkers from which water had to be pumped. Waiting for a clear moment on the runway, we trundled across to one of the bunkers, only to find it empty. Fortunately, another nearby one still had water in it. The bunker cap was removed and the hoses from the fire truck were laid out to transfer water. An argument ensued as to how the hoses should be hooked up—after all, we were going to suck water into the truck, not spray it out as we would if we were quelling a fire.

About fifteen minutes later, the argument settled, hoses were connected to the right valves and the pump activated. There were now about ten of us standing around, scattered among the coils of fire-hose. When the truck's powerful pump was started, the hose rapidly filled with water from the sump, stiffening it, sending the coils writhing and the bystanders jumping to avoid becoming victims of a canvas boa constrictor. This was a colourful scene that could well have been accompanied by a spirited calypso.

It took some time to fill the truck with brackish water. Meanwhile planes kept landing and taking off for the ninety minutes that this whole operation took. It left me wondering how many times the truck had actually been used and what might have happened with an untimely crash. Every time thereafter that I flew out of Beef Island, I cast an eye to the fire shed where that truck was parked, wondering if it had its full supply of poisonous retardant and sump water. I knew the crew was ready.

That knowledge turned out to be of marvelous comfort on my next flight out on American Eagle. After a long wait in the airport holding room, we ambled out onto the tarmac and into the twin-engined plane. I settled into a seat on the right-hand side, looking out the window at the engine nacelle. I soon noticed a substantial leak of aviation fuel, running from the engine onto the hot tarmac. It pooled there, iridescent in the sun, evaporating slightly less rapidly than the drip. I was contemplating a flight reschedule when the pilot did his walk-around and noticed the pool of kerosene. A debate ensued. A group formed for discussion purposes. Alternatives were proposed. This could be a cold leak, in which case it would cease when the engine heated up at take off—or it could be a hot leak, in which a fire in flight was a possibility. Meanwhile the leak continued.

Not wishing to miss their schedule, the pilots decided that it was a cold leak and we could safely take off for Puerto Rico, some forty-five minutes away. As we revved engines for our turn onto the runway I could see the airport fire truck in its shed, crew standing by, and was mightily relieved. That turboprop engine was about three feet from my window and I watched it for every one of those forty-five minutes.

At the Feet of the Mighty

The human resource planning seminar at the Prospect Reef Hotel in Roadtown dragged on into the swelter of late afternoon. Outside the open door, only feet away, the holiday sailboats careened past, spinnakers filled with the trade winds, while I droned on. The lights and air conditioning were out due to a power failure in the island's diesel plant. I was instructing the Cabinet and senior public service of the British Virgin Islands on a July afternoon and I was ready for a rum and coke and a swim in the sea.

The day was filled with discussion of the government's long-term development ideas for BVI's position among the tax havens of the world. The Bahamas, the Channel Islands and other aspiring Caribbean nations were the competitors. Banking rules, discretion and financial expertise were the subjects of planning. Of course, the eight hundred civil servants also had such issues as dismal salaries, promotion barriers, training needs and the prevailing nepotism inevitable in such a small nation of fourteen thousand people. With me that day was the leader of the opposition party, but absent was the Chief Minister, Lavity

Stoutt, who was in bed at home, convalescing after an operation on his big toe.

As BVI is a British Protectorate, still ruled nominally by a British Governor, Lavity was a *Chief* rather than a *Prime* Minister. Despite this distinction it was clear whom the islanders regarded as their proper leader. I recognized the potential gaffe in holding a strategic planning session with the opposition leader, without the chief, so I offered to visit Lavity at home the following day to bring him up to date. When I reached his home I was greeted by a maid and sent along to his bedroom. Can you imagine visiting a head of state with such gentle security?

What greeted me as I entered his bedroom was a huge, cast-enclosed foot. Lavity was reclining, elevated by pillows at both ends, but his pillow-supported foot was the first thing I saw. His greeting was cordial and we soon got to talking about the substance of the workshop. I had also noticed fluorescent bumper stickers in town saying "Support BVI Community College," which led to a discussion of his aspirations for the young people of the island. There were many who said that BVI was too small, that there would not be enough students, that they could never find the money, that it would not be recognized in the academic community, that no one would want to attend. During my time working with BVI islanders I helped to devise the inaugural curriculum; Lavity built the college, now named after him, and it is a going concern. He is one of my heroes!

His favorite biblical aphorism, "without vision, the people perish," illustrates the man. No one should have doubted either his resolve or his ingenuity. A favourite story surrounds a campaign promise he made in seeking his first mandate as Chief Minister. The island of Tortola lacked a highway route from north to south, blocked as it was by an area of sheer cliffs falling directly into the sea—Lavity would build it! The island lacked the equipment to engineer a road through such an obstacle and most people scoffed at the idea. But BVI was a British Protectorate, often visited by ships of the Royal Navy. Lavity prevailed on one Captain to assist him. The ship shelled the cliffs for much-needed gunnery practice, the sappers of the Royal Marines blew the pathway, and Lavity had his promised road.

Eugenia Charles of Dominica was, by contrast, most definitely the *Prime* Minister of an independent state. A lawyer by profession, she was the unchallenged political leader and matriarch of the Dominican society. She ruled the island with a completeness that was legendary. Very little occurred that she had not planned or sanctioned and certainly nothing occurred that she did not know about before or shortly after. One vision of her sticks in my mind particularly. She and President Reagan are standing together for the television cameras. Reagan is announcing the invasion of Grenada to save Western Democracy and Eugenia is supporting its necessity.

But it is the more personal and direct vision of her that I am to recount here. I was on Dominica, giving another human resource planning workshop. For visiting dignitaries representing a foreign granting agency, an audience with herself was definitely required. Aubrey Armstrong, my Caribbean colleague, and I were to appear promptly at 10:00 a.m. to be properly introduced and, I dare say, screened. The entrance to her tiny law office was as unguarded as Lavity's bedroom. As we were ushered in the door Eugenia did not stand to greet us, for protruding through the tunnel of her desk was a large, much creased, bare-toed foot at the end of a cast. She had broken her leg and could not stand without help in extricating herself from her desk. We spent the entire interview on wooden chairs, separated by the foot. Our meeting was cordial and her insights into the needs of the island nation were, of course, astute and precise. It was becoming clear to me, however, that meeting Caribbean leaders was to be placed at the feet of the mighty.

In a later visit to the island, as Ed Sutherland and I were conducting a workshop, the head of the aid project decided to visit Dominica. He landed at the main airport, declined taxi service, and wandered across the island, sightseeing on foot for most of a day before checking in with us. It was the following morning that he appeared to the assembled trainees, expecting to be revered and celebrated for his ambulatory prowess. When our organizational counterpart saw him and heard his story, his black face blanched to white. Eugenia had not heard! He was in trouble! She was not aware that the head of the aid project was on Dominica—and, more importantly, he had not paid his respects as would be anticipated and should have been arranged in advance. Our counterpart bolted from the room to tell her and to arrange the necessary protocols, his morning shot. Within the hour a request came from the Prime Minister suggesting an immediate audience. Our dear project leader was quick to comply, interpreting it as a measure of his personal importance. We knew better and so did Eugenia!

Zim Dollars

What do Central Bankers talk about over lunch?

Near Windsor Castle, along the upper Thames, we assembled central bank Governors from ten southern African countries. The old manor house was a scene of understated luxury appropriate to the task. Our project was designed to assist the bank staff in developing their systems of debt and reserves management. This particular occasion was designed to give the Governors a "hair down" session—a frank exchange of goals, methods, tribulations and triumphs. Among those assembled were the Governor of the Bank of Zimbabwe, a participant, and the Governor of the Central Bank of Argentina, a resource person brought in for the occasion.

These were the people who minted the money, advised Presidents, and decided whether to pay the World Bank loan instalment today or to plead with the IMF over restraint policy. Their policies on currency exchange or money supply could beggar the masses or keep a struggling economy alive in the face of discriminatory trade. With all this weight on their shoulders they of course felt it necessary to travel first class in separate limousines from Heathrow, secure in their isolated importance. Not to say that they were not down-to-earth—it was just that they printed the money after all!

Lunches were where we heard the truth. Over smoked salmon, truffles, *pâté de fois gras*, medallions of spring lamb, vegetables julienne and fresh fruit, washed down with chardonnay or Perrier, the stories started to emerge. It seemed that most of their currencies were printed in other countries in order to reduce the temptation for workers to divert the product before it hit the streets. For example, the Zimbabwean dollar, which can only be used in the country itself, is printed in Argentina and shipped in containers to Harare. Given the exchange rate for Zimbabwean currency, it takes container loads to meet the local demand for circulating bills. It appeared that one of these containers had been hijacked by a group of thieves somewhere along the shipping route. I thought that this would surely have caused some concern for security. In fact, the Zimbabwean and Argentinean bank Governors nearly choked on their coffee cake as they laughed uproariously about the intelligence of crooks who would make the mistake of stealing Zim dollars—and outside the country to boot!

While the laughter subsided another story was building at the next table. The project had sponsored a workshop with the Governor and staff of the Bank of Lesotho. Work was going well in the Lesotho meeting, but the atmosphere in the country was a trifle tense because the police were on strike and the issue was building toward a messy climax. At 11:45 that morning, the doors to the meeting room burst open and in marched a squad of submachine-gun-toting police. Was this the end of the seminar? Was it the end of the project? Was it the end of the Governor?

It seemed that the police had read in the paper that morning that the government simply did not have the money to pay for their exorbitant salary demands—an understandable bargaining ploy—and took this literally. As payday was the next day in Lesotho, the police were very upset that they might not be paid—an expectation that seems a bit out of character with a strike, but it is hand-to-mouth in Lesotho. The squad frog-marched the Governor out of the room and slammed the door behind them.

All was quiet in the room as Ed Sutherland and his group of facilitators checked their travel documents and the bank staff thought about the safest routes back to their villages.

As it was lunchtime anyway, the group broke the session, agreeing to reassemble at one o'clock and wait for developments. As they nervously waited, the doors opened once more to admit the Governor, in one piece and smiling mischievously. The police squad had taken him to "see the money." They wanted to see the central bank vault and would not be satisfied until they could see that the money needed to pay tomorrow's salary was actually there in a heap of bills and coinage.

Some Governors live a little closer to the people than others.

All this story-telling had its effect. When the Governors left to return to their countries, they shared limos to Heathrow.

The Mango Tree

Philippino forester Dr. Lucrezio Rebugio was philosophical about it. He had just been maneuvered out of the Presidency of the Asia Pacific Association of Forest Research Institutions by the suddenly-expanded Indian contingent to the annual meeting in Kuala Lumpur. It was an organized coup and it upset Luc's systematic rise from Vice-President to President, which we all expected. The APAFRI executive had proposed Luc in their slate of nominations as the logical successor to its first President, Dato Dr. Salleh Moh'd Nor. They were blind-sided. You could sense the conspiracy in the room before the election: the room was filling up with Indian delegates, people who had never before shown interest in the affairs of the organization.

The newcomers may not have been knowledgeable about the work of the association, but under the constitution they had the voting numbers and they had been briefed. Behind the delegates, feigning disinterest, was a man given to damning by faint praise, the Indian Executive Director of a UN agency that saw APAFRI as a an interloper on the international forest research scene. The buzz was that APAFRI's growing slate of successful programs had been captured by Canadians and had to be rescued. Elected as President was a Malaysian of Indian extraction, a good man to be sure, but an old rival of Dr. Salleh and his successor at the helm of the Forest Research Institute of Malaysia. The old order passed democratically in form, but it was a coup nevertheless.

It would have been perfectly fitting for Luc to be President, for he had a cosmopolitan grasp of Southeast Asian forestry, a history of international development and experience as a research leader. At home he was Dean of the Faculty of Forestry at the University of the Philippines in Los Banos. His alumni were in forestry faculties and research institutes all over the region—we found them in Vietnam, Cambodia, Malaysia and Thailand, every one of them delighted when Luc came on the scene. On the podium he was an accomplished speaker. As an executive member of the association he was a quick study and a man who tended to say yes to proposed innovations: exactly the man to build a multinational fledgling organization.

Debriefing later in a hotel coffee shop, I asked Luc if he was personally hurt by the coup. No rancour, no bitterness, just his gentle philosophical nature emerged as usual. "Disappointed, of course, but not hurt," he said, all too familiar with the machinations of academe. "In a way it is a credit, not a loss... there is an old Philippino saying: 'People do not throw rocks at the mango tree unless the fruit is ripe.'" This demonstrated perfectly the class that we had come to respect.

How To Break In a Pathfinder

I had been traveling the province with Sarah Doe, of the Ministry of Small Business Tourism and Culture, promoting the development of Tourism Gateway Communities. As winter approached we began renting substantial 4x4s so that our tender coastal feet were properly ensconced in a cage of big iron.

As was our custom, we made a pre-Christmas trip to the Valemount Gateway ("Our Valley in the Mountains") in a candy-apple red, brand spanking new Pathfinder, rented from Budget in Kamloops. This was a fine machine, with only 5K on the clock! I say, *was*.

We traveled uneventfully through the Darfield corridor to Valemount, enjoyed our time in that exciting community and left in the dark hours of a snowy Saturday morning for the return trip to the Kamloops airport. After a couple of hours of mushing along the slushy, compact-snow-covered highway, past Mike Wiegele's principality of Blue River, we descended into the valley of the North Thompson River near Clearwater, where the snow cleared and the road stretched out straight and dry (we thought). It was December 18, 1999.

In relaxed cruise mode, well in time for our flight, we anticipated an uneventful run to Kamloops. Surprises were in store. Without warning, our rear end (the Pathfinder's, that is) started to drift sideways. I corrected in the prescribed manner, turning with the skid, but the four wheels of our marvelous machine had grown wings and an independent mind. We skated gracefully over the crown of the road, which we found later was glare ice covered with a skim of melt-water, and began our rendezvous with the North Thompson River.

We left the road as I bleated, "hang on!" and Sarah closed her eyes. We hit the roadside berm of snow sideways, missed a power pole by six inches and did a convincing barrel roll over the edge, bouncing once on a stepped bank and ending up on our side in a shallow, ice-covered branch of the river.

When the world stopped turning, I noticed that I was hanging suspended in my seat belt with a fine view of the river and that Sarah was doing the sidestroke in a foot of water. For some reason she found this unacceptable and asked if I wouldn't mind getting her out of there before I wrote the accident report. My first practical thought was to see if we were sinking or not. No, the water was not rising beyond Sarah's shoulder. My vision was blurred and my left eye felt wet. I said something like, "I think I've lost my eye...Oh well, it's just my left one," to which she replied, "Could we just get out of here now?—and stop your whining, I'm cold!" At that point I noticed that the airbags were hanging like spent balloons and that the motor was still running. There is no stopping a Pathfinder! As the cab was beginning to fill with steam, I decided to turn the engine off. With no wheels on the ground I figured we might have to walk anyway.

We did manage to clamber out the driver's side door—now the roof exit—slither over the snow-covered side, sit on the left rear wheel and eventually jump into the foot of water and wade the three feet that separated us from the bank of the river. We did all this under the watchful eyes of a growing gallery of passersby who repeatedly asked if we "needed any help," to which we replied several times, as we struggled out of the roof hatch, "Of course not: we are just breaking in our Pathfinder." They seemed convinced by this because none of them came down the bank where the snow and then the water were over street shoe level.

They did say that the police and ambulance would be along shortly, and couldn't we just wait for the proper authorities like any other accident victims? Eventually they did help Sarah slide over the bank, up to the road and into the waiting RCMP car where a very kind officer lent her a sweater and turned up the heater to slow Sarah's violent shivering.

In the meantime, I removed the sodden luggage from the partly-submerged Pathfinder and heaved it up the bank to the waiting multitude of dry people. That stuff was heavy, being full of Thompson River water. I needed the diversion at this point, so I didn't complain about doing this cleanup work. Although I was a consultant on hire, I wasn't charging for this time. Sarah's official black government briefcase was the worst of all as it held water for the rest of the day and had to be drained at the hospital, where they have procedures for such things. Probably this has something to do with government security.

We were asked for our driver's licences, home addresses, Care Cards, reason for leaving the road without permission, and intentions with respect to fishing out of season. Oh yes, and what happened? The RCMP officer, the driver of the ambulance, the paramedics in the ambulance, the hospital entry clerk and the nurse all asked for this information so we are sure we got it right eventually.

As the ambulance trundled us back toward Clearwater, the paramedics went into their securing routine. I was sitting in the jump seat and Sarah was laid out on the gurney. At first they tried to fix a neck brace but had trouble finding one short enough. "Get me the no-neck one," the attendant said, endearing himself immensely to Sarah. He then told Sarah that they would have to remove her cold, soaking wet jeans—and, by the way, her underpants. The peeling process was quite arduous and I did my best to remain concerned but unobservant. He then said, "I'm afraid we will have to remove your cold, wet bra as well," to which she replied testily, "I'm *not* wearing one" with enough fervour to ensure that the disrobing process was terminated. As they noted my concern, and my comforting hand placed on Sarah's cold cheek (the one on her face) they asked me, "Are you married?" I said no, we were just colleagues, but the question lingered.

As for me, the front seat attendant decided to measure my blood pressure as a matter of precaution. I was off the scale at a systolic pressure of over 200, which caused them to speed up the ambulance, fearing that I was about to expire. Actually, it was just my normal reaction to crashing a Pathfinder into the Thompson River, nothing to get upset about.

The Clearwater hospital received the two of us like honoured guests. They were glad to have us alive, unlike some of the others that had been admitted that day from the same patch of road. Sarah was taken off to be X-rayed to see if all her parts were still appropriately connected, while I was merely asked if I could see the doctor's finger when she held it behind my ear. I supposed that this was a form of reverse discrimination but decided not to raise the issue just then. My nurse said, "It's great that you are bald. it makes it easier to clean the blood off your head." I was both comforted and flattered that she had noticed.

The X-ray technician asked Sarah repeatedly if she was pregnant, making sure that the procedure was not going to cause inadvertent damage. After the third time this question was asked, Sarah burst out, "I'm not married, I have no partner, of course I'm not pregnant!" The nurse answered, "Well dear, after all, this is the time of year of the immaculate conception." When Sarah told me of this exchange in the recovery room later, my internal voice said, "Well, I could fix that." It was irreverent of me, of course.

As I was beginning to contemplate a day off the consulting trail, in bed with solicitous attendants, I was evicted from my emergency bed to make way for a more recent arrival screaming, "It was not drugs, it was just a lot of lousy beer!" The waiting room was OK but my luggage was leaving pools of river water on the floor and it was hard not to get my dry socks wet.

Our wonderful RCMP officer drove us to the Greyhound bus depot for the trip home. As the bus drove past the site where we went off the road, Sarah turned to me and said, "I guess we're angels now!" Indeed we were much more, but could not know it then. We were married in May 2004, but the important vows were non-verbal and were exchanged in the Thompson River, while breaking in a Pathfinder.

Lara of Africa

My daughter Lara is great traveler. When she was eight I took her to China on an expedition to Xian. The trip across the ocean was a long fourteen hours and she was a cranky brat by the time we reached Beijing. Our hosts whisked us to our hotel as they could see what was needed. Lara leapt into the bathroom and I turned down the cover on her bed. To my horror the pillow was alive with cockroaches. I heard the crash of the bathroom door and the rapid footsteps, slapped the pillow and swept the roaches down the wall at the head of the bed. She jumped in and was asleep in seconds. This was the definition of a narrow escape!

In Xian we met Wang Jing Lung, the foremost artist of the "Peasant Painters" group. I managed to purchase fifteen of his paintings and coveted many more. He offered to trade paintings for Lara, but the transaction was vetoed by her, even without calling home to mother for advice.

On a second occasion, I gave Lara the choice of Barbados or Yellowknife in January. To my amazement she chose Yellowknife, saying, "I like winter," not knowing that fifty below is different from Victoria's wet snow and west coast chill. Before we left Victoria I tried to get her to understand that she would need more than a t-shirt and a rain shell for arctic conditions. Have you ever tried to talk a teen-ager into wearing a jacket? In Yellowknife our hosts arranged for her to go on a dog sled ride. I can still picture the scantily clad girl, bundled under caribou robes, having riotous fun in the lurching sleigh but shivering until her teeth rattled.

Our great African trip together was to Zimbabwe and it was another exhausting flight. Now she was sweet sixteen and "cranky brat" no longer applied. That does not eliminate other possibilities, however. Before leaving Victoria I had advised her to accept a robust packsack for her belongings, knowing as I did the rigours of baggage handling on international trips. Like the arctic attire debate, this too led to an alternative choice. She selected her favourite pack from school, well worn, zipperless, faded and ready to burst from the accumulated CDs, duplicate clothing and other inexplicable necessities. On arrival in Harare airport, Lara stormed off the plane in a daze, heading for the terminal before I could get out of my seat. I followed her, retrieving the trail of belongings that were strewn along the aircraft stairs and across the tarmac to the terminal door.

When my development work was done, we headed off to a safari in Hwange National Park where our accommodation was a thatched cottage on fifteen-foot stilts. We went into the bush at five in the morning, seeing the full range of savannah animals, elephant, giraffe, hyena, fox, wildebeest, impala among them. At night we heard the scuffle of a nearby lion kill. In the morning, over breakfast, we watched a baboon troop cavort in a meadow. When it came time to depart she burst into tears at leaving this unforgettable scene.

Compensation followed quickly, however, because our next stop was Victoria Falls on the great Zambezi River. The Victoria Falls Hotel was a colonial marvel. Spacious rooms, high ceilings, languorous fans, potted palms, starched linens, elegant silverware and English breakfasts were quite a contrast to the bush camp we had left behind. For the tourists there were nightly drum and dance performances, redolent of the jungle. I can still picture Lara of Africa, standing alone, perilously close to the edge of the cliffs overlooking the thundering falls, wreathed in mist, transfixed.

The African drums got into our blood. Back in Harare, we selected a heritage drum, topped with impala hide and carved from a hollow tree, to send home. The National Museum was selling a few of its artifacts to raise money to tend its extensive collection. Back in Victoria some months later, an enormous crate was dropped by crane into our front yard. We pried it open, extracted the drum and brought the sounds of Africa to the unsuspecting Oak Bay neighbourhood.

James of Thailand

I was introduced to James before I met him. James was on an agricultural exchange between Canada and Thailand when Sarah and I got together. He spent a few months on an Ontario farm and then went overseas for the reciprocal farm experience. My first vision was of a handsome young man riding into a Thai village on the back of an elephant, thronged by admiring maidens and welcoming villagers. Not a bad image.

All I knew for sure was that Sarah was very proud of his adventure and that she was anxious for his return. Having been to Thailand myself, I fully expected him to return with one of the admiring maidens or, failing that, a small elephant, but that was not to be. His future would see him married on horseback instead.

Alexander of Valemount

Alexander and I travelled by train from Vancouver to Valemount, the same excursion route that had become necessary for Sarah and I after I ruined our vehicle in a winter drive and was prohibited from risking her life for the foreseeable future. We enjoyed champagne in the club car, elegant meals on railway silver in the dining car, watching life go by in the dome car, and bunking among the swaying curtains in the sleeper. We stepped off the train in Valemount to a set of boring meetings for which Alexander showed amazing tolerance. The next day held more promise.

We headed out by snowmobile up into the mountains with a guided tour. Along the valley floor tracks, both of us on sleds for the first time, we lurched from side to side until we had mastered the steering and got our bearings. Then it was up the mountain trail in increasing depths of snow. We emerged into a trackless sub-alpine basin, by then cocky experts. We blasted around the basin, jumping snow-covered logs and testing the maximum speeds of the sleds. Surprisingly, Alexander did not wreck his rented machine, despite his extraordinary record with cars, vans and trucks.

Emily of Albion

Emily has inherited the determined adventurousness of her mother. Together they have travelled to Britain, Holland and New York. They were beset by monkeys at Longleat Estate in England, toured Stonehenge, rode the London Eye, elevatored to the top of the Empire State Building and eyed (but did not join) the pot smokers of Amsterdam. This trekking began one day in the Florence Lake house. Emily had stated categorically that she was "going to go to England," while her mother was distractedly working on the home computer in her office. I overheard the ensuing conversation, went into the kitchen and phoned Air Canada. Before they had finished their discussion I had booked their flights. I returned to the office and told them to get their passports and money ready and pack their bags.

This first excursion to Europe began a tradition of mother-and-offspring travels—Emily was hooked, so how could the others not get their turns? Sarah took Alexander to Scotland to introduce him to a proper appreciation of Scotch. She took James to Las Vegas and Death Valley on a photo shoot. A lifetime of stories was harvested from these trips, just as I have collected mine, one to one, with Lara of Africa.

Saying No to Noor

King Hussein of Jordan was one of those truly remarkable men who rightly captivate the attention and respect of the world. Head of the Hashemite dynasty, he ruled the Kingdom of Jordan from his late teens until his death, earning global respect for his integrity and balance at the centre of one of the most volatile parts of the middle east. Hussein's wife, Queen Noor, was equally revered by the world for her kindness, intelligence and beauty. An American by birth, Queen Noor had made an enormous adjustment in joining the royal court in Amman. Like her Jordanian-born counterparts in the Royal Family, she was active in public duties, sponsoring and supporting many of the non-government organizations that provide so many of the development initiatives within the kingdom that could not be achieved by government alone. She is widely revered by the common people of Jordan.

I was the external evaluator contracted by World University Service Canada for the King Hussein Environmental Management Training Project. I was commissioned to conduct a mid-term evaluation. The project was designed to train Jordanians to conduct environmental impact assessments for industrial projects in the country. Targets of the training included government officials, industrial personnel and members of non-government environmental watchdog organizations. The project was well set up and functioning as effectively as any I had ever seen—my report was extremely favourable.

I was asked back near the end of the project to perform its summary evaluation to file with CIDA, the ultimate funding source. The Jordanians had made extensive use of the training, both in Jordan and in Canada, and had implemented impact assessments throughout the country. It was one of the best examples of technology transfer that I had seen as an evaluator. The Jordanians were so happy with the project that they were advocating a two-year extension to consolidate the gains. Enthusiasm and expectations that CIDA would respond favourably were very high.

Over one hundred participants, from all the project's sectors, were present at the last scheduled event of the project, a seminar on environmental policy conducted in Amman. Queen Noor was the guest speaker, acknowledging that the project was named after her late husband. It was exactly one year after the death of King Hussein. When she rose to speak, she began with a memorial salute to her late husband, with a breaking voice and immense dignity. She pulled herself together and, showing a clear grasp of the project and its importance to Jordan, praised the outcomes and the work of both Jordanians and Canadians in achieving such success.

At the end of the event, she came down off the stage to mingle with the organizers of the seminar and to thank them personally. To a tight knot of project and government officials, of which I was a part, she said, "If you will continue the project, I would be willing to act as its Royal Sponsor. Please let me know within the next two weeks." It was an offer that no respectable development agency could possibly refuse.

CIDA did. The moment passed. The Canadian government did nothing. The project lapsed. We said no to Queen Noor on the one-year anniversary of the death of her husband, King Hussein of Jordan.

Last Day in Jordan

One week before, terrorists had blown up the Marriott in Jakarta. Today, I was sitting in the lobby of the Marriott in Amman. Storm clouds were gathering over Iraq and young men in the streets were beginning to cast angry sideways looks at white foreigners. A Canadian is just an American in such a situation. As I sipped my coffee, I could not help but glance at the lobby windows, the placement of the pillars, the proximity to the front door, wondering how the shattered glass might be distributed...

I had been working in Jordan periodically for five years, evaluating college development and environmental management programs for the Canadian International Development Agency. In this last phase in the year 2000, I was working with the Minister of Education, Dr. Khaled Toucan, developing a national education strategy. How could we get conservative village families engaged with the design of public education? How do we link the schools with the work place? How can we link the high schools with the emerging system of community colleges? It was the stuff of development to which he was intensely committed.

Dr. Toucan tended to stoop apologetically, out of modesty, like many tall men, not wishing to intimidate shorter people. He exhibited an intelligence sharpened by his scientific training, an aura of authority expected of a senior Cabinet Minister and a sense of humour that leavened the weight of his responsibilities. He was a physicist by training and a member of one of the elite families of Jordan, and thus a perfect candidate for being executive government. Jordan is ruled by the Hashemite Royal Family, now under Hussein's eldest son, King Abdullah, but is also governed by an elected parliament that works with the Royal Family in a unique form of democracy. Thus the ancient tribal interests of Jordan are served while the balance-wheel of elected officials deals with a growing public of worldly sophistication. The Cabinet, however, is selected by the King, not necessarily from those elected to the parliament. That is how Khaled Toucan became a Minister, drawn away from his professorship at the University of Jordan, appointed by the King to ensure not only that the ruling class was represented in government but that government was also led by those truly competent to serve.

I had finished my final report and presented it as a Canadian perspective on what might be the future trajectory of secondary education in Jordan. Dr. Toucan had welcomed the Canadians working in Jordan, at one meeting exclaiming forcefully, "I could easily have the Americans, with all their money, but I don't want them—they will force their agenda on Jordan. I want the Canadians: they will help me do what I want to have done." It was a reminder to me about the necessary ethic of the development consultant, working across the cultural divides.

Now, this was my last day in Jordan. My flight was booked for the morning and it was clear that it was time to close the chapter as the tensions were beginning to destroy the sense of benign acceptance that had been my reception in the country. I was ushered by attendants into the spacious office of the Minister. Dr. Toucan waved me over to the little square of couches in the corner of his office, motioned to his servant for tea, and cleared the office for our last conversation. We ranged over the years in Jordan, the several projects worked on and the outlines of the national education strategy paper just finalized. The audience was drawing to a close when, with a chuckle, he strode over to his desk and picked up a paperback book.

He was insistent: I must read this book. I should find one and read it on the plane. The title? It was Michael Moore's *Stupid White Men*. It was his parting comment on the difference between his Canadian colleagues and his American suitors—something we could both laugh about.

Of course, being Canadian, I have often wondered if my own work in Jordan might have justified such a parting gesture...

Going to the Wall

The machine gun chattered—the revolution was over. Citizens, jubilant to that moment, poured, instantly panic-stricken, over the fortress wall, down forty feet into the bush-cluttered rocks and the upper streets of St. Georges. The forces of Bernard Coard had just executed Maurice Bishop and Jacqueline Creft, abruptly ending the enlightened leadership that was flowering once more on the Caribbean island of Grenada.

Ken Braveboy, Principal of the Grenada Technical Vocational Institute, was the head of the local militia unit that had freed Maurice Bishop, the revolutionary Prime Minister, from house arrest. Enormously popular, Bishop was paraded through the streets of St. Georges, gathering a growing crowd of deliriously happy Grenadians. The throng wound its way up to the colonial-era hill fort overlooking the city, expecting to take over the garrison and reclaim government from the murderous gang of usurpers that had seized the country by armed coup months before.

Looking behind him on the winding, hilly street, Ken saw an armored car approaching, firing its machine guns indiscriminately into the crowd. As the vehicle sped up the hill, he dropped to the pavement and rolled aside, lying under the traverse of the guns. When it passed he jumped up and ran behind it, frantic that the celebrating crowd, now inside the fort, would not be aware of the danger until it was too late.

He could not run fast enough. Ken reached the entrance to the courtyard of the fort just in time to see Bishop's group hustled around a corner and up against a wall. They were shot where they stood, without ceremony or mercy, and the hopes of a renewed revolution died there in the pools of their blood.

The crowd was desperate to escape the slaughter now that the guns were trained on them. They ran for the fortress wall and scrambled to the top, flinging themselves by the hundreds over the wall. That evening, at home in Nanaimo, I watched the human deluge pour into the rocks below, horrified by the television images of a familiar place and people in such agony. We did not know then that Ken Braveboy, our counterpart educator, went over that wall with the others, breaking a leg but surviving to tell us the tale.

Jacqueline Creft was the Minister of Education. Only months before she went to the wall, I had interviewed her on behalf of Malaspina College, which was delivering a technical training program to Ken's institute on behalf of the Canadian International Development Agency. She met our contingent of college educators in her drab, olive-coloured revolutionary fatigues, coming out of her office with a determined stride, visibly conveying her distaste for nonsense, emphasizing how little time she had for educational theories. She called us comrades, the jargon of the revolution. When we plied her with our great plans for technical training she tilted her head and replied, "When I have achieved universal primary education on this island, I'll talk to you about post-secondary programs!" The asperity was for effect and she followed the admonition with a serious discussion of the long road ahead and her dreams of giving Grenadians the educational opportunities they needed and deserved.

Things large and small were lost that day in 1983. When Jacquie went to the wall, she took Maurice Bishop's unborn child with her. Ten years later, on the national day of commemoration, I sat in the Prime Minister's office with Permanent Secretary Gloria Payne-Banfield (who was Minister of Planning in the revolutionary government) and wept alongside her in remembrance. The sadness lingers still in Grenada.

iv *reflections*

Old Bones
Zen and the Art of Motorcycle Camping

Getting down onto the mattress
Was easy enough at first,
Although the last few inches
Were more like a controlled fall—
Graceless, but with a loud sigh
Of contrived satisfaction it was possible
To make the agony sound like ecstasy,
Drown out the popping of the knees,
And have the collapse look planned.

The centimeter of space-age foam was hyped
As the ultimate in camping comfort:
Providing insulation from the damp
Preventing the hips from reaching the ground
And generally suspending the camper
In blissful ignorance of the terrain.
Ideal for dreaming of the rainstorms
Pounding on the tent fly—
Another perfect camping invention.

Lying on my back ogling the tent roof
And making amazed noises at the comfort—
Willingly suspending my disbelief
In the obviously spurious claims
Of the manufacturer's marketing firm,
I rolled over onto my side
Only to lurch onto the pebbly forest floor
Lying immediately under the tent:
The terrain said to be impossible
To feel through the amply advertised thickness.

It was not just the tilt of the earth
On which the tent was pitched,
Or the centrifugal force of the turning planet
Or a sudden desire for privacy...
It was the width of the mattress
Which had obviously been made
For anorexic twenty-somethings
Of scant weight, girth and length
Who do not snore when constrained
To sleep on their backs the whole night.

If it were not for the cervically correct pillow
That kept my spine in the approved position,
The presence of a spouse-like bolster on my right
That prevented rolling in that direction
And the motorcycle packs and boots, axe,
Flashlights, helmets, water bottles, leather jackets
That were piled on my free-rolling side—
Why, I might have been in another campsite
When the morning sun finally, finally
Warmed these old bones.

Air Raid

On VE day, May 8, 1945, I was standing on the Monterey Street sidewalk in Oak Bay, just outside the elementary school fence and just under the red pole lofting the air raid siren when it went off signaling the end of the European war. But the real ending took place on the first hour of July 29, 1944, when the Halifax bomber carrying my father Gordon and eight other men crashed on the playing field of the village of Antrim in Northern Ireland. When I was fifty-five I visited the crash site in Antrim and his grave in a churchyard on the Aldergrove air base.

I had such a sympathetic and helpful reception from the local people that in three days I learned all that was truly important about that time in 1944, and as a result wrote this letter to my Irish friends.

September 18, 1995

To My Irish Friends:

Since I returned home I have been mulling over my experiences in those few days in June of 1995 in Co. Antrim. Each of you chose to help me reach into the past to recover the memory of my father and to connect parts of my life that were severed in 1944. What I have come to cherish greatly is the generosity of spirit and the deep level of personal understanding that you showed for me and that now seems uniquely Irish.

What I found collectively was a respect for the continuity of history and family that took as a given that a man of fifty-five would be deeply moved by standing for the first time at his father's wartime grave. Each of you materialized that understanding by taking action to help me find people, places and things that might have escaped me in a brief three-day visit. I found a well-cared-for grave, a bomber's crash site, and the written record. More importantly, I found people who understood the sacrifice made by those young bomber crews and who had not forgotten them. I found people who live with the memories, walk the cemeteries, collect the artifacts and live in full knowledge of what was won and what was lost.

This part of my letter is deliberately addressed to you all so that you will understand what a remarkable picture of the Irish spirit I took away.

Maggie Smith started the chain on a Friday afternoon by hearing my questions about an Aldergrove archive and taking the trouble to find David Whiteside, who was born in the chaplaincy building in which she worked. David listened to the nature of my search and went home to dig through his files, finding Eddie McIlwaine's article on Corry McBride.

"I have found an article with your father's name in it." There was Corry kneeling at my father's grave! I tracked Corry down and telephoned him like a voice from the past. Over lunch the next day he and his wife Florence painted in the details of a remarkable story of coincidence and deliverance. From Corry's photographs I found out that the roses flanking Gordon's grave were yellow. My last act on the Monday morning before I left was to cast a yellow rose on Sixmilewater.

The dry official correspondence lead me by myself to the crash site on the grounds of the Antrim Forum. There I talked to men who were curious ten-year-olds when the crash occurred and who pointed out the open ground and remembered when day broke on the morning of July 29, 1944, when they came to see what remained of the Halifax and its crew of nine young men. Along the Sixmilewater I found Jim McGarry, Skipper of the Maid of Antrim, who gave me coffee below and put his mind to the people who might know more. He led me to Ernie Cromie, President of the Ulster Aviation Society, who had personally catalogued the piece of Halifax DT642 that had been found by divers in Sixmilewater. Ernie spent a whole Sunday evening with me rooting through the Society's hangar, showing me the collections and the aircraft restorations, and looking for an elusive piece of airframe. He also took me back to the Forum grounds to point out the faint gap in the trees where the bomber tore its swath on the way to the ground fifty-one years ago.

On Sunday I attended services at St. Catherine's on the Aldergrove Base. There I was noticed among the wartime graves by Canon Musgrave who invited me in and introduced me and my purpose to his congregation. It turned out to be their Trinity Sunday Tea, to which I was also invited, meeting Mary and Eileen over lunch, ladies who have visited those graves, sorrowing over the youth of the occupants. I know they will return from time to time, acting like members of my family. After the service, Canon Musgrave's son drove me down to the hangars at Langford Lodge and the nearby headquarters of the Aviation Society.

I talked to Eddie McIlwaine of the *Belfast Telegraph* to let him know the far-flung influence of his thoughtful article.

I phoned Maggie Smith to let her know how her compassion started the chain of connections. I met David Whiteside at the airport on Monday, where he came to see me off, and I could give him the outlines of this story. Now when I think about each of you and all of you together, I think that it is to Gordon Fraser's eternal good fortune that he lies among such friends.

I include in this letter two poems, written on the Saturday and Sunday evenings. They share with you the thoughts and feelings that you helped to shape. Please accept them as my personal thanks to each of you and all of you together.

Sixmilewater

Fully loaded for a night over the Atlantic,
Halifax DT642 heaved uncertainly into the air.
It carried nine young airmen
Of Heavy Conversion Unit 1674.

For days it had been defying mechanics,
Refusing to take on its standby crew,
Giving them thirty six hours of boredom—
And, incidentally, their lives.

The lucky ones stood down to make way
For the final crew on their last mission,
Anxious to complete their training,
Full of confidence in their own skills.

They liked the Halifax for its reliability:
A forgiving plane for long distance over water
Made to take the heavy weather over the sea
Reporting storms and chasing submarines.

Did they have any misgivings that night?
Probably not the volunteer on board,
Gordon Fraser, who went along with a buddy,
For company, on his last training flight.

One more than the usual eight-man crew,
The nine men buckled in and concentrated
On the instruments, controls and radios
That were their preoccupations and their duty.

Just into the air the trouble began—
Power was strong, but there was no lift,
No response to the pilot's urgent attempt
To gain the normal altitude for nearby hills.

Fast and level for three miles they flew
Before the Halifax began to sag toward
The low wooded hills and the village,
Antrim, asleep and trusting on that summer night.

They were coming down, no doubt,
So, banking into a shallow left turn
The Pilots, Lenz & Edwards, took them round
On a desperate try for Aldergrove.

There is a memory in the Massereene Wood
Where that clapped-out old bomber
Tore through the darkened trees
On its way to the ground.

It is of nine men on their last mission,
Trapped in a failing airframe,
Knowing their last moments were near:
No time for a last letter home.

There was enough fuel for a night over the Atlantic,
Enough for a full-scale funeral
With light reflecting off the trees
And the ripples of Sixmilewater.

Nine young men's spirits tend that wood,
Though official graves were set for them.
Children play there now and old men walk
Who can see the spirits, and the flames.

I Have Found You, Gordon, My Father

I have found you, Gordon,
My father, amid saxifrage and daisies,
Irish sun casting rose-leaf shadows
On your headstone.

I have found you, Gordon,
My father, waiting at St. Catherine's,
Hard by the flight line
These fifty-one lonely years.

Have you been anxious that I
Would never find you here,
Your only child, unaware
Or oblivious to your hidden place?

Your name lives on in me and mine.
It stands, written, looking out to sea,
Oft visited, near the home where they sent
The one-line telegram and your wings.

Your modest grave in Ireland
Has been kindly tended by workmen,
Respected by comrades,
Catalogued with care by officials.

Forty-five airmen lie at your side
Neatly placed, backs to Lough Neagh,
In a corner of the churchyard
Where the afternoon light gathers.

Your gravesite is washed by the smells
Of jet fuel and manure from the fields,
The warplane and the ploughshare
Ever competing for supremacy.

You lie in the Aldergrove RAF Base,

Just off the runway
Where your Halifax made its last
Take-off roll into the night.

I run my hand over the letters
On the face of your stone,
Chiseled admission by authority
That you were but twenty-nine.

"I will dwell in the House of the Lord,"
Says the face of the stone
Rooted firmly in the soil
Of the village of Killead.

Lying next to you is your crew-mate:
Like a younger brother is Len,
Looking up to you in question
From his age of twenty-two.

"He gave his life that we may live in peace,"
Says the face of his stone—
Though he might well wonder
At the sounds of Aldergrove today:

The roar of jets is constant;
Intermittent small arms fire,
I hear from the practice range,
As patrol helicopters clatter overhead.

My route to your two graves
Was guarded by youths of twenty-two
With automatic rifles slung
And fingers on the trigger guard—

Helpful youths who eased my way,
Maybe sensing the full circle
That I represent for them, and I,
Old enough to be their father.

A bright, crisp flying day today,
Perfect visibility over land and lough.
You would savour the chance to fly
On a day like this, wouldn't you?

How different from the wee hours
Of July 29, 1944, when your Halifax
Hit the trees of Massereene
And ploughed into Antrim's ground.

Oh yes, I have found you, Gordon,
My father, your spirit tangible still,
To add to the kind image
I have always carried while you were gone.

I am your son, Bruce,
Who stands beside you thinking
Of all the sharings foregone
And the rebellions I could not try.

Go peaceful, Gordon, my father—
I needed to find you but this once
For it to be forever.
This honour I pay you, at last.

Estimates of Calibre
Reflections on a Meeting with the First Nations Summit, March 2004

People are quite careful in the presence of auditors who may yet pay them a visit. While they might wish to complain in private about the flagrant biases of investigators, to question the parentage of the Board Chair, or to remark on the auditors' dim understanding of the industry, they are by and large quite polite to our face. Finding out what they really think is a rare opportunity...

Many non-replaceable tenures are being granted to First Nations by special agreement as part of the Forest Revitalization Program of the Ministry of Forests, some for a share of available AAC volume, some specifically earmarked for fire and pine beetle salvage opportunities. Under the Nisga'a treaty, the Nisga'a Lisims Government took over management of all forestry activities within their treaty lands on May 10, 2005. With the opportunity for an economic development boost and a position in the forest industry comes the possibility of being audited by the Forest Practices Board. For the Nisga'a people, self-government means that they may well have to invent their own audit processes to be assured of the sustainability of their operations.

On March 10 and 11, 2004, Dave Mannix and I made a diplomatic visit to the First Nations Summit in the big house on the Capilano Reserve. Our intention was to offer the interest of the Board in working cooperatively with First Nations that are acquiring timber tenures and finding themselves under scrutiny for their forest practices or who, on obtaining treaty lands, may wish to develop their own unique systems.

I made the formal offer and then Dave took over. With a knowing wink to me, he waxed eloquent about the value of the Board. As he warmed to the task, our capacity to serve grew to amazing proportions. The climax came when he suggested that the resort to the courts increasingly sought by First Nations was ruinously expensive. "Why not use the Forest Practices Board?" asked Dave. "It would be a lot cheaper!" I remained silent. Who was I to diminish the capacity of the Board in public?

We were received very cordially. Polite questions were forthcoming. A decent interval ensued before our time at the table was brought to a close. In his final remarks, thanking us for our efforts and our good intentions, Grand Chief Ed John summed up our value with this memorable phrase: "Yes, ladies and gentlemen, having the Forest Practices Board on your side is like having a derringer in your boot!"

It was instructive to have our calibre so succinctly estimated. It reminded me that for our shot to count, it must be carefully aimed, delivered by a steady hand and fired at close range. It is a credit to Keith Moore, the inaugural Chair, and Bill Cafferata, my predecessor, to say nothing of their armourers and scribes, that although a small instrument, carried quietly among the shotguns and howitzers of government and industry, all whom I have met remain wary of the impact of a well aimed FPB report.

Hello Nose!

Eddie the dog could always tell the sound of our motors coming in the driveway and was wagging up a storm at the window, nose pressed against the glass, as we came up the steps. From tongue to tail her whole body was in motion: the greetings of absent pack members caused a moment of delicious chaos. Sometimes it was accompanied by an immediate need to water the flowers, sometimes just a demand for biscuits to tide her over until dinner. The *click-click-click* of her nails reverberated about the kitchen, up and down the hall, and back around for another tour to use up the excitement she had stored up over the day. She hovered until the human food scraps were poured over her sawdust pellets, which she then wolfed down with abandon. The problem with those human food bits was that they seemed to promote gas, which we could make her feel embarrassed about if we complained enough. If "Oh, Eddie" was uttered in a strongly disapproving tone, she would slink into the basement for a while, knowing full well the problem she had created.

Eddie had a history of breaking out of confinements. She began life as a street dog, unconfined by modern conveniences like closed doors or carrying cages. She is reputed to have eaten through the floor of a closed bathroom and completely destroyed a steel carrying cage, and has without any doubt defaced every closed door in the Florence Lake house, inside and outside. She was happiest during the long days when she had the full run of the house and, particularly, the living room couch. If we had inadvertently forgotten to padlock some garbage, she helped herself to that as well. We are uncertain about the full scope of her actual diet, comprising as it did kibbles, highly-flavoured pizza box supplements, soft drink cups, yogurt containers, chicken bones and rotting things normally sequestered under the sink. She ate everything that James, Alexander, Emily and their friends declined to eat immediately and burgers they put down on accessible plates. She knew when the people-snacks or chocolates had been improperly stored at a low enough elevation. She had a nose for such things.

One of her many peculiarities was her reaction to family hugs. Whenever such a display was seen she would bark menacingly until we quit. We never knew whether that was a reaction to conflict or to being replaced as the centre of attention. Anyway, it was a good indicator if there was any covert smooching going on among the youngsters!

Her favourite walks were in the local parks, where she vastly multiplied the human mileage. Off the trails in Thetis or Francis King, her nose worked overtime, covering acres of smells as fast as she could run. If there were other dogs present she tolerated them for a second or two before attacking them for their presumption that the smell banquet was theirs to share. We had to carry a weapon to beat off the snarling jumble of otherwise placid dogs. As she grew older, after such a romp she had to be helped into the car and would sleep for two days on reaching home. She believed that she still was a puppy, or maybe a teenager, but arthritis had begun to set in and the proverbial Labrador back end was giving out.

She reacted the same way at Shawnigan. Out of the boat and up the ramp, nose going at full tilt, she had to inhale the whole island before settling down to a mere paddle in the weeds. Her frequent visits to the humans left wet, sometimes muddy paw prints on every available surface, just to make sure we knew that she was there. Her "water dog" credentials had to be renewed on each visit, either by swimming from shore or by leaping off the dock to join the swimmers, dog paddling away, gargling the lake and snuffling in time with her paddling front legs. At the end of the day, she was comatose on the front porch, wrapped in towels, hardly able to move. If she knew we were heading for the lake without her, she would unleash her most plaintive howls.

When we constructed our sun porch, we installed a porthole at dog height. It looks over the front steps and gave her a barking platform. Besides looking like the front end of a mounted specimen, the back end of which looked equally odd, she could surprise delivery people with a ferocious bark and growl routine immediately above their right shoulder as they reached for the mailbox. If only we could have turned her loose on the neighbour's black cat, the one that pees on our motorcycle pipes. She was certainly willing, even eager!

Often her morning would begin when Eddie heard us making the coffee from the basement and she came up for a fast pee in the yard and a biscuit to start the day. When I was sitting in my reading chair, she would lay her head in my lap to have her ears rubbed, her neck scratched and her shoulders massaged. When breakfast was done and we were on our way to work, it was a quick trip to the dog walk along the lake, for her characteristic two pees and a pooh. If only this were her only location for ablutions.

In Eddie's later years her copious bladder, refilled regularly from the white telephone, and her considerable digestive system contributed to the ambience of the Florence Lake house. Nary a carpet, floor, nook or cranny was unadorned with the products of her metabolism. When we tore out the basement wall-to-wall carpet, it was disgustingly saturated. We could have established a mushroom farm! We took to buying cheap Home Depot specials that could be laundered or chucked. We purchased case-lots of paper towels and floor cleaners. We became adept at mopping before breakfast and upon returning home. Alexander walked a basement minefield each morning, not daring to paddle around in bare feet without the lights fully blazing.

Entering the front door after work, we instantly knew the news. Another "Oh, Eddie!" would be followed by another slink into the basement, the rapture of our return being dampened by the odour of her greeting. We took to blocking off a few places to prevent the worst; she had learned to force the lock on our upstairs bedroom, where a comfortable bed was located. We could not imagine her offerings being left on the little Turkish prayer carpet. But she compensated by protecting the house, aggressively barking at delivery people and other intruders.

As Eddie turned thirteen, around eighty-five human years, her systems began to falter. Her friends and family provided her with raised dishes that she didn't have to stoop over, with health-food fit for an aging dowager, with comforting toys; she was walked frequently with hopes of emptying her preemptively. Her occasional lapses in sanitation became chronic. We were voted "most valuable customer" by the paper towel company. Her X-rays showed a tumour that occupied her belly so fully it deformed her diaphragm into her chest cavity. Her muscles were still good for chasing cats, her eyes were still acute, her nose was as discerning as ever, but her hind end was dissolving. We asked the vet, "Is it time to put her down?" She replied, "No one would blame you for doing so," but we tried medication first—it proved to be inadequate. Eventually she became worse. Alexander's mine field had become a swamp and we could smell the house from the Spencer Shell Station at the turn-off to Florence Lake Road. Her caretakers were beginning to despair. It was time.

On Eddie's last day, Emily showered her with tears and took her for one last walk along the Florence Lake pathway. Sarah, Alexander and I prepared the car for her and she jumped into the back seat with her usual joy at being included. She could not know the destination, but we did. We drove in a car made of lead for the few blocks to the clinic. She jumped out as enthusiastically as ever and pulled at the leash to get into the clinic, where the cornucopia of smells was both familiar and exotic. Her somber family accompanied her into a small clinic room, where the quietly sympathetic vet explained the procedure and took her away to insert a catheter in her leg. When she came back into the room, she settled onto a folded comforter and the vet introduced a mixture of tranquilizer and opiate painkiller. Eddie relaxed into a drug-induced calm, with her head in Alexander's arms. The vet then told us that the next injection would be a lethal dose of the anesthetic they used for surgery and that it would act quickly. He warned that her bladder and tract might relax and release, but we were so used to that in daily life that we could not have been bothered—besides, it was his blanket.

The vet injected the last dose and Eddie, ever so slowly, gently, laid her head down and was gone. We stayed with her for a while. We wept. We still do.

Goodbye Nose.

A Tryst at Noon

First, my kimono-like garment was slipped above my knees. Then Gladys, with a deftness reminiscent of a Subway sandwich maker, waggled her squeeze tube, drizzled warm gel on my testicles and smeared it around. Her expression was one of professional detachment, but I knew this was exciting her at least as much as it was me. It must have been the way she had me wrap my penis in a towel and hold it out of the way that was the clue. I believe the towel was to obscure any inconvenient erectile responses and to keep any visual cues from affecting her resolve. As she manipulated her instrument, I focused my attention on the video screen, fascinated, voyeuristically, by the play of images.

"First I'll do the right one," she said, "and then I'll do the left one." This was more detailed attention to my equipment than I had been led to expect, but, you know, I take these kinds of pleasures where I find them. Where I found them, of course, was the ultrasound ward of the Saanich Peninsula Hospital. It all ended too soon, this lunch hour of abandon, with Gladys saying, "You can wipe yourself with that towel and get dressed now," as she rushed off to share the steamy pictures with her man friend, the radiologist. Wow! What a professional: worthy of a scene from *Memoirs of a Geisha.*

For some time now, my right testicle has been sending pain signals, often at the most inopportune times. It is OK to flinch in public, but usually you are able to express the reasons to those who witness the event. You can picture the scene: "OUCH! Oh, it's not your fault, I just have a sensitive ball—you couldn't have known." Not exactly elevator conversation.

My doctor, intending, I believe, to ameliorate worries, suggested that these sorts of pains are quite common in older men. "It could be that you are drinking too much red wine or eating too much chocolate," he said, adding one horror upon the other. He went on to say that he had seen this sort of thing often in the weeks after the Calgary Stampede. It seems sore testicles are common among short-term cowboys who sport those tight jeans during Stampede week and compress themselves into later agony. Makes you rethink the story of Brokeback Mountain.

What is much worse is contemplating the potential surgical response to all of this. What if these signals are cancer in the making? What if they suggest an orchidectomy? (What a diverting euphemism that is!) Already I can hear the column of British soldiers singing "Hitler has only got one ball, Himmler's are surely much too small, Goering lost his to whoring," to the tune of the Colonel Bogey March. I would whistle along if I hadn't withdrawn all of my breath already. What is even worse is that this marching song ends with the punch line, "And Goebbels has no balls at all!" I can hear the stamping of feet and the sharpening of bayonets eager to fulfill the prophecy.

Christ, worse yet is the image of the guardian of the harem. Oiled, generously muscled, girded in loin cloth, scimitar at my belt, formidable in appearance—but bloody useless, and I don't dare raise my soprano voice to admonish intruders.

The verdict, until the technicians have ogled the films, is that nothing could be found which should be leading to hurt. Well, Gladys should know: she sure poked around enough and must have seen a few balls in her time. Of course, she could have been referring to that timorous shrinking member hiding in the towel...

I believe that the ultrasound examination is referred to as a non-invasive procedure. Well, they didn't poke any holes to collect bits of ball or ram something semi-electronic into an orifice, which is a definite consolation. But if I were to see those video images plastered on the net, I bet I could make a case for invasion of privates. Although anyone actually seeing Gladys in action would probably just click onto the next porn site in search of something a little more invasive.

A Ghost at the Reunion Table

I would like to share a discovery about the wisdom of attending reunions, particularly those of a spouse.

Mine was part of a particularly satisfying graduate student team as she pursued her advanced degree. As is normal in such circumstances, the team, under pressure, bonded like a platoon of soldiers at the front. They developed their own language and rituals, became each other's confessors and in due course set in place the intimacies of the well-oiled group. Wonderful—one of the great experiences of depth in human affairs.

So, as the spouse at home, enduring the gap in companionship and minding teenagers who were using the absence of their mother as an opportunity to ignore their pseudo-parent, the bonding cycle at college was for me more like being inside the spin cycle in the now all-too-familiar washing machine: while it is happening it is a confusing kaleidoscope of perception even though the purpose is to come clean. I could see and hear the team bonding taking place, celebrate her opportunity and at the same time soak in the wash cycle of despair that our relationship would be taken to the cleaners, washed away, replaced by more exciting fare. Actually, it was more like being holystoned, that process whereby small rocks remove the top layer of wood on the deck of a wooden ship to make it white enough to please the captain!

So I endured, chafed, cried, paced and, on occasion, drank. None of that worked, of course. But it eventually ended, graduation gowns were paraded, job prospects were elevated and erudition abounded about the house. How could one grouse about that? After all, that was what all that agony was intended to produce, wasn't it? The long hours of study, the nights at the computer (me in the cold bed alone), the frantic team meetings to plot the next assignment, the meeting of deadlines, the production of insights for professors of limited wisdom—all these were necessary grist to the mills of the masters. But there was another residue.

The bonded team entered e-mail heaven and promised to meet for reunions—to relive the high moments on the front lines, to savour the hard-earned intimacy, to "use the network" and to carry the torches of relationships created. And torches there were. Well, guess what? The washing machine still worked! That old spin cycle was alive and well, the main squeeze was again submitted to the wringer for good measure—just to make sure that none of those earlier tears were left in the fabric. Mentioning such fears, by the way, is not a good thing to do! It spoils the well-earned celebration and tears are seen as rain on the parade.

So time passed, we returned to a state of companionship, projects were built, wine supplies laid in for the winter, dance lessons taken, motorcycles purchased and ridden into the sunset. Phew! For a moment there I thought that once I had been washed and dried it would be time for the storage closet where the old, boring, threadbare fabrics were put. Well, it didn't happen, but when the washing machine starts up in the basement some days there is that momentary ripple of cold that runs up my spine, unbidden and uncalled for.

So, the reunion. The grad student team, now in mid-career success mode, sets the date for a grand get-together. A great location by a lake, a couple of days to swap stories and supplement the email traffic over a few bottles of scotch—a replay of a nightly ritual developed to space out the evenings of heavy-duty assignment production during the residence weeks. Can you picture it? I couldn't, because I offered to go along!

The team assembles in a round of excited hugs, exclamations, enquiries over missing cohort mates and the insider shorthand that only the team knows. There I am, right in the middle of it but right out of it at the same time. Around me swirls the commerce of the team. It is in a different language, exclusive, rapturous and opaque. People are spoken of whom I have not met. Lives are dissected in which I have no stake. Relationships made, broken and mended are exchanged as the normal currency of the team. I am bankrupt, not so much as a farthing of information in my conversational pocket, so I adopt what I hope is seen as a pleasantly approving smile, a kind of active silence—hoping that it does not freeze into what will appear to them a condescending grimace over the hours I must wear it. I lapse into personal reverie, I make many trips to the washroom to look into the mirror to assess if I have in fact, gone invisible. Nope, just figuratively.

Occasionally I am addressed in person—"How is your supper?"—but it is a sudden courtesy of the slightly embarrassed, not a real question, and the exchange is over before an answer is given. They use my wife's pre-marriage name. I recoil. I eat rather quickly, because there are no pauses for conversation. My wine is exhausted rapidly because I sip it regularly as a semblance of participation. Pictures are passed around, but not to me, because it is obvious that I wouldn't know the subject anyway. Sometimes I am asked a real question in a field I am supposed to know about, but my voice has atrophied and I croak out some cryptic half reply as though awakened from a deep sleep that began in another century when people spoke in monosyllables and wore skins. These courtesy questions to the outsider are well meant, but the chatter quickly moves back into group shorthand, duty done.

Eventually I crash. I know what it is to be sent to Coventry. I now understand fully why primitive villagers found this a more effective form of torture than burning at the stake. It harnesses the fears of the shunned, which, in the silence of social disengagement, magnify into demons more terrible than any the real world could produce. Men who are "just friends" become sexual rivals on the make. Every happy gesture, every peal of laughter, every innocent and gaily exchanged bit of gossip or intelligence is taken as another milepost on the way to Coventry—or toward that back shelf in the closet of time.

Then I act! Crash those gates, wrest the spouse aside and bitch annoyingly. Dig up the resting past and fling it about in petulant rage. Create a distraction from the group love-in. Walk on the other side of the road, make distance an ally in the retribution, be brittle in reply, and at least temper a bit that exclusive happiness from which I feel so excluded. Making a fool of yourself is at least visible and auditory—even if the audience is short lived!

As the event winds down, there is relief from me and visible reluctance to part among the others. This extends to an email trail by Blackberry even as we travel down the highway toward the resurrection of the home. "Damn, will nothing be as fulfilling as that bloody team? Is that male friend more than he seems? Did I just see the tip of the iceberg?" Those demons sure know how to get to a guy! And that Blackberry would make a terrific sound as it hit the gravel margin!

So there it is, my friends. If you are thinking of inviting your partner to your reunion, don't! If you are the one thinking of making the magnanimous gesture of going along to your partner's reunion, don't! You can't get there from here. If it is your reunion you will be distracted from the pleasures by guilt or mayhem created by your self-destructing partner. If it is your partner's reunion you will pollute the well of their pleasures while riding that spin cycle towards Coventry—it's no wonder Churchill allowed it to be bombed!

And if, perchance, you are a university professor designing intensive team-based programs without thought for re-entry—then you, especially, should be forced to go to your spouse's team reunion.

Landfall's Last Sail

Twenty-nine years ago I moved onto *Landfall*, moored at Canoe Cove. It was October, the days were filled with autumn light and my adventure with the sea had begun. The ensuing winter saw snow on the deck, ferocious southeasters hammering the marina, and perilous docks covered in ice. It was great down there in the saloon, fire going, rain pounding on the tarps, and the rum rations plentiful.

Spring came with a honking flock of Canada Geese, sailing in the gulf islands and the libations of an ever-enthusiastic crew. *Landfall* graced her way into classic boat festivals; tried to sink the *Oriole* on a sail past; was dressed in expensive finery of new sails, new engine, new stove, new cabin sole, new rigging, new anchor, refurbished decks, rebuilt rudder, a succession of heads and endless bottom painting; and sent lots of cash to the bottom.

Cyril Rodd was *Landfall*'s builder, and her keel was laid in 1965 at his boatworks in Sidney. She has a hidden compartment to foil thieves and customs agents and a gimbaled table built by one of the Rodd sons. It was his own boat, an Atkins design, made stoutly for offshore cruising. The doghouse on *Landfall* was designed by Bill Garden and has that characteristic "eyebrow" that leans into the sea ahead. *Landfall* traversed the Panama

Canal and tasted Caribbean water under his captaincy. Legend has it that Cyril was given his nickname, Twink, by Emily Carr for whom he had done errands as a boy. At a classic boat festival, Mary Rodd, Twink's widow stepped on board and wept tears of remembrance on the deck.

Landfall sailed with me into Desolation Sound, spent many nights at anchor in Irish Bay, took green water over her bow, sailed with her scuppers under, ghosted on her head sails, dragged into the docks in Friday Harbour and fouled on the coast's largest derelict anchor in Pender Harbour. She smells of old salted wood, crabs in garlic butter, Lagavulin, diesel and curry.

She launched a bushel of potatoes into the sky. She was been boarded by the RCMP. Maidens danced on her portlights and masked men in her hold. She hosted parties, some of which can be recounted in polite company, some that resulted in disgustingly drunken sailors and some that lead to weddings.

She moored at Canoe Cove, at Boat Harbour, at Fulford Harbour, at Tsehum Harbour and at Maple Bay. She ran aground on Sidney spit, bounced on the docks at Fulford in a full gale, thrummed on her anchor line in a northeaster at Prevost. She discovered Pot of Gold Coffee on Thetis Island, made ceviche in Telegraph Harbour, was saluted by cannon, hosted College Presidents, tested man-overboard gear on a hypothermic crew member, comforted a baby seal, steamed a sackful of manila clams, and ran by night into Secret Cove to avoid a sudden night wind. She has watched the fireworks at Butcharts Gardens, the amateur anchoring dances at Clam Bay and the zodiac races in storm-wracked Pender Harbour.

A host of supplicants gave her a face-lift on her thirtieth birthday. Her saloon reverberated with the wails of Linda Ronstadt, the percussion of African drums, the folk songs of Kate Wolf and the stories of errant sailors told in flickering lamplight. She met blue water sailors returning from afar, bringing young lovers together. Men and boys jumped naked off her decks. She towed girls in a zodiac a hundred giggling feet behind her. A wedding party was stranded on her in Ganges Harbour, and she greeted Septembers in the still waters of Tod Inlet.

She has been a home, an office and a retreat. Her complement of masks has been retired but her aura remains. She is aging now, with signs of softening in some of her timbers, some clogging of her through-hulls, some greening of her rigging, some vibrations of her engine and discoloration of her sails. But on our last sail together, in April of 2009, she put her rails under and laughed at the southeaster rushing into Cowichan Bay. She has been given to the Cowichan Wooden Boat Society, where a group of older men are caring for the artifacts of a disappearing culture. Sarah and I left her there. She looked wonderful.

Ed Sutherland noticed that she had left her berth and wrote:

Bruce

I noted the absence of the lady on a recent walk to Maple Bay Marina and subsequently spotted her in Cowichan Bay. There was sadness at the moment of realizing that she had passed on.

Seeing her in Cowichan Bay, I paused and recalled the many occasions when those decks and below provided opportunities for escape, joy, friendship, solitude and inventiveness. She provided the venue for the start of a new life for Craig and me; she provided the introduction to the rest of the sail gang; she was the impetus for the purchase of the Loon; and she provided the venue for the first time I met Ingrid.

A very special lady. Here's to her!

The Moral Majority

When I was sixteen, my Anglican mother took me to a séance at a mansion off Oldfield Road in Victoria. We ground up the long driveway in her 1953 Austin Somerset to meet a few others who were intent on reaching the other world that evening. The group gathered in the musty drawing room, clustered around the circular table, the lights dimmed. The medium entered the room. She was elderly, dignified and calm, exuding the confidence of the truly connected. She greeted us solemnly, asking each of us what we desired to communicate across the cosmic divide. She concentrated deeply, letting the silence rule the group, until the atmosphere was thick with expectation. She helped some of the devotees reach departed loved ones, both thrilling and comforting them with messages drawn from the benign ether.

Finally she came to me with a question. "Do you have anything you would like to ask of the spirits?" she asked, condescendingly, of the only youth at the table. I thought for a moment and asked, "Why did Christ on the cross say, 'My God, why has thou forsaken me?'" She was not pleased with this direct and difficult question and the séance ended with a bang. She was exhausted, she said, the lights went up, tea was served, and the issue was quickly forgotten as an aberration in an otherwise satisfactory excursion into the afterlife.

Religion was always, for me, as much a question as an answer. But the search for a greater scheme of things in which to place my allegiance was bubbling over during my days as an undergraduate in the Botany Department at UBC. By accident I discovered the literature of the "Moral Majority," a popular movement from the States that sounded like a place to cache my idealism. I was not aware of its rightwing fundamentalism at the time. Fortunately, I wrote a letter to my Aunt Eileen, herself a leader in an international Christian organization called The Infinite Way, expressing my interest in joining the movement and, more fortunately, she replied. "There are some," she said, "who will dedicate their lives to doing moral things, and then there are others who will spend their lives tilting at windmills." I was not exactly familiar with legend of Don Quixote, but I knew what the expression meant and, getting her drift, steered clear.

My next attempt was to approach the local Anglican Church, just down the road on the campus grounds, which advertised an active youth group seeking new members. I appeared spontaneously at a scheduled youth meeting, wandering into the midst of a clique of very well acquainted West Point Grey youth, clutching their silver spoons. The group reacted with an intake of their collective breath. What was this outsider thinking of in crashing their open meeting? Did he think that the youth group was open to just anybody? I explained why I was there, the nature of my quest for a centre of moral purpose, but my voice trailed off as the stares grew blanker by the moment. I beat a disdainful retreat in short order, leaving the group to their developed comforts.

Blunted in seeking the medium-assisted enlightenment, the popular movement and the organized religious options, I returned to the focus of my studies—slowly absorbing the new science of ecology as the touchstone of a moral approach to the world. Again, by accident, while browsing in the bookstore, I ran across Bertrand Russell's book entitled *Why I Am Not a Christian*. He demolished the validity of the orthodoxy of organized religion so eloquently that it permanently cured me of both my Christian upbringing and my search for moral certainty in the dogmas of the church.

So, where did that leave me? What was to be the true north for my moral compass? Was training in science going to eradicate mystery and spirituality, leaving only the products of the laboratory? Were ephemeral hypotheses and cold, scientifically derived evidence all there was?

Gradually, what emerged was a new synthesis. Humanistic, naturalistic, pragmatic, but respectful of the intricate natural world that the ecologists of the day were trying to understand. At this stage in my life, some fifty years beyond the séance table, I am inclined to see the world the way that Lovelock conceives of it in his Gaia Hypothesis: the world is a completely integrated ecosystem, full of constant change, cycling idiosyncratically from one massive disturbance to another, always righting itself within the limits of habitability by the interactions of living things and the physical world. Humans are just one organism in this wildly unpredictable mix and we must come to the position of humility that our situation demands. My fear is that we have reached the status of sorcerer's apprentice and are only able to cast industrial spells, the consequences of which we can neither imagine nor reverse!

So, if there is a moral centre for me, it is to be as benign a factor in the ecosystem as I can, while still engaging in the human commerce of my time. No monuments, please. No attempts to build lasting artifacts, just the eventual return of all that I am into the timeless experiment of the living earth, glad of the experience, thankful for the placement in a brief period of plenty, expecting only the fleeting memories of my friends and loved ones before they too are cycled into the ever-changing combinations that evolution creates out of our elemental and chemical components.

If this is all there really is, stripped of all the explanatory fictions of human artifice, then all that matters is how one chooses to live—what dedications, what kindnesses, what reverences for living things, what stewardship of nature can be mustered within the culture to which we were born. It is not about faith in the fictions, it is about reverence for the whole, magnificently improbable earth and the life it has invested in us for the time we have been given.

www.ingramcontent.com/pod-product-compliance
Lightning Source LLC
Chambersburg PA
CBHW032001080426
42735CB00007B/466